T0195854

GRIEVING SUICIDE

ONE WOMAN'S JOURNEY THROUGH THE SHADOW OF LOSS

Karen M. Atkinson, MA, CPC

BALBOA.PRESS
A DIVISION OF HAY HOUSE

Balboa Press books may be ordered through booksellers or by contacting:

Balboa Press
A Division of Hay House
1663 Liberty Drive
Bloomington, IN 47403
www.balboapress.com
844-682-1282

Because of the dynamic nature of the Internet, any web addresses or links contained in this book may have changed since publication and may no longer be valid. The views expressed in this work are solely those of the author and do not necessarily reflect the views of the publisher, and the publisher hereby disclaims any responsibility for them.

The author of this book does not dispense medical advice or prescribe the use of any technique as a form of treatment for physical, emotional, or medical problems without the advice of a physician, either directly or indirectly. The intent of the author is only to offer information of a general nature to help you in your quest for emotional and spiritual well-being. In the event you use any of the information in this book for yourself, which is your constitutional right, the author and the publisher assume no responsibility for your actions.

Any people depicted in stock imagery provided by Getty Images are models,
and such images are being used for illustrative purposes only.
Certain stock imagery © Getty Images.

Print information available on the last page.

Library of Congress Control Number: 2022910644
ISBN: 979-8-7652-2964-4 (sc)
ISBN: 979-8-7652-2965-1 (e)

Balboa Press rev. date: 07/08/2022

CONTENTS

INTRODUCTION

When I began putting together the ideas for this book, I spoke to a few colleagues and friends to gauge their thoughts on publishing a book about suicide. Suicide is not an easy topic to talk about, and to be honest, writing a book was never in my plans. I was not the author in the family; my parents were. Yet something was propelling me forward. I picked a few friends, women who were not only strong but were honest and critical if necessary. I expected cautiously supportive responses. Perhaps it was a topic they couldn't really relate to. Maybe someone would suggest I take a class on how to write a book.

I knew they would speak openly, and they did. With each conversation, I did not get feedback about choosing this difficult topic, nor did I get feedback about my writing. Instead, I was privileged to hear, for the first time, the untold stories of the suicides that occurred in each of their families. Unexpected tragedies. Suddenly, out of the blue and seemingly with no warnings, their loved ones took their own lives. They were unexplained, random, and shocking deaths. From there, the responses were universal. "I wish there had been a book like this when I lost my brother," and, "I didn't know who to turn to or who to talk to about it after it happened. I'm so glad you are writing about this." Suddenly, our conversations were filled with universal mourning and the experience of loss from devastating suicides.

Those responses reaffirmed this book. They were also responses that broke my heart. I thought back to how many years I had known some of these families. So many years had passed, and I was only now hearing about this. Because my ex-husband committed suicide, I was experiencing what they had experienced. I was being invited into a very private space. When asked if I could share their family stories, almost all declined. This is the shadow of suicide. It holds shame, pain, and sometimes a lack of reconciliation. There is deep loss and often the need for privacy. It becomes a family tragedy that leaves an uncompromising ending and unfinished legacy. It also holds a forbidden topic in our culture. Very few speak openly about suicide.

In the years since Tom's passing, there has been a series of teenage suicides in central California, putting police and support teams on alert to make sure they did not become "cluster suicides." Then quiet reports surfaced in our neighborhood about three suicides of students from the high school, just a few blocks from our home. With the press quiet, news spread through conversations with parents and students in the parking lots of schools or at sporting events. Brief mentions. So many losses, so many suicides. Too many. And on the public front, suicides of celebrities like Chester Bennington, Avicii, Kate Spade, and Anthony Bourdain. Public suicides, echoing this trauma, reminding us, life is precious, and sometimes people suffer in ways we simply can't imagine. It can be hidden, dark, secret. Each shocking, each heart breaking, and each unexpected.

Over these years, I have learned a few things about those who have lost a loved one to suicide. I have learned that the way people die can be just as important as the fact that they died. And that death by suicide is traumatizing. I discovered very little was written about this community of survivors. After a tragedy, the natural tendency is to focus on the person who suicided and the shocking event itself, forgetting those left behind. But there are family members, friends, colleagues, and a community who live on after the loss. And they must learn to carry this tragedy with them in their everyday lives.

More important, they often need support after the fact. I've learned that there can be judgment around suicide as a choice for death, such as the Christian and Catholic beliefs that suggest those who suicide do not go to heaven but to limbo or hell instead. The truth is that we don't really know where souls go. But still, existential fear pushes forward outdated belief systems as a natural way to defend against fear of the unknown.

Suicide is a topic that needs continuous discussion and open dialogue. From the "You just need to get over it," perspective to, "Just be grateful for what you have and think about the future," I think there can a better shared perspective. One with less judgment and need to fix. When we connect and share our stories with others, we bring this difficult topic into the light, where it needs to be. Our voices bring understanding and compassion. There are so many who suffer alone after they lose a loved one in this way, and it doesn't have to be that way. Those left behind need ongoing support and community more than ever.

For the loved one left behind reading this, I wrote our story for you. I may not know you or who you lost, but I know something terrible has happened. Something devastating. Something that has altered your world forever, and it is hard to move on. So in these pages I have written about my experience—our experiences—to help us all move forward and connect as a community of survivors.

I closed my mouth and spoke to you in a hundred silent ways.

—Rumi

CHAPTER 1

THE CALL

According to the Centers for Disease Control and Prevention, there were 42,770 suicides in the United States in 2014. These statistics included a 49 percent increase among men between the ages of forty-five and sixty-four. More recent research has shown that children, elders, and men in their forties continue to be the most at-risk groups for suicide. I sought out these statistics after my ex-husband killed himself. He was forty-four.

The call about my ex-husband's death came late in the afternoon on a Thursday as I was getting ready to head out the door. He had called at 1:30 a.m., waking me up from a horrible nightmare. As I was waking up, the call went to voice mail. Tears streamed down my face, and I could hear myself soothing him in my mind, rocking myself back and forth, saying, "This will pass. Things will get better. You can get through this. I love you." I didn't understand what was happening. Little did I know at that moment, five blocks away, my ex-husband was killing himself.

There's a book out there I'm trying to track down. It's about seven people who jumped off the Golden Gate Bridge and lived to tell their stories. Each one reported that as soon as their hands hit the railing, they regretted their choice. I think about that night and our intense connection. I wonder if he had that last moment of regret. On October 2, 2014, my ex-husband committed suicide. And I still can't believe it.

It had been a strange day for me. Waking up like that in the middle of the night had left me feeling off all day. It was like I moved through the day in slow motion. I left work early, thinking I was coming down with a cold. As I walked to my car, the first call came in from our oldest son.

"Hi, Mom. Dad was supposed to pick me up. I am here in the office at school waiting for him."

There was a short pause and then, "I thought you said Dad was supposed to pick me up."

Then a long pause, followed with the click of a button.

An alarm bell rang in my head. The reality was that the person I had been married to all those years, the one who had been such a great husband and who was loyal and dependable, had disappeared due to a serious methamphetamine addiction. As he changed and became more volatile, we separated. As the addiction grew, and the possibility of saving our marriage disappeared. The result of the addiction and the changes that followed were hard on all of us. I constantly felt myself shifting my point of reference from the person I had known for so many years to this new guy I didn't recognize. It was a guy who wasn't always nice or predictable. I held hope this was simply a phase that would pass. We had recently turned a corner, or so I thought. After a few years, the divorce was finalized. He had started to appear clean and sober more often than not. The great job he had lost was replaced with a new one. I knew we weren't totally out of the woods, but he was trying.

The concern in the back of my mind was that he would not admit to the addiction—a serious, deadly addiction. With anger management, drug testing, and therapy, a judge finally forced him onto a path of recovery. It was just two years too late. I held hope because we needed him. I needed him as a coparent and the father of our children. He was a primary attachment for them and irreplaceable. The children were young and didn't understand what was happening.

I guess I was hoping after a few rough years, we would get a chance to start over, to turn a new page. He had recently regained custody of the kids and had a new job lined up. The house had finally sold, and we were finalizing the divorce. Things appeared to be OK, not great, but OK. We were finally moving forward. Baby steps. We would formally be a divorced family, functioning as co-parents. We'd have to learn how to be friends again and put the kids first, like we had for so many years before the addiction.

I was also hoping he would get back to the way he was. That guy was a great guy. I wanted him to start showing up again. But that was not meant to be. As I drove straight from work that day to pick up our son, I thought about the man I had married. In many ways, he made marriage and parenting easy. He showed up for years. That guy was nice, friendly, social, responsible, loving, and so involved. He loved life. When the addiction kicked in, there were no signs initially; there was no money missing from accounts, there were no little bags of white powder in secret stashes, there were no beady eyes or trembling hands. There were no calls in the middle of the night or outbursts and no visible stages of detox. All I had was a feeling that something was off. In the very beginning, all I saw was some unhappiness with his job and a lot of fatigue from all the work travel. We had just buried my mother and were both dealing with losing my parents that year, emotional stressors that set the stage for a storm to start brewing. I saw grief in response to loss. They were big losses for both of us as well as for our family and friends. We were saying goodbye to two people who were close to our hearts.

As I walked my son back to the car, I remember feeling a sense of dread. Tom had become unpredictable, but he would never miss a chance to be with his kids. And today he just had. I ran through my memories for clues. When the judge released Tom, he immediately called me. We talked, having an open and honest conversation, both feeling hopeful. I was his first call, which I thought meant something. With his release, the restraining order had been lifted, so I asked if he could watch the boys. After all we had been through, for me to ask him to watch the kids that evening meant I was still willing to help him keep those relationships. The olive branch had been extended. We were both trying to move forward for the sake of everyone.

I can tell you that he loved his children. Losing the marriage was hard on him, but loosing custody was the knife in his heart. I had hoped it would be enough to get him to stop using. Even with the growing addiction, the subsequent raging, and all the anxiety, he loved our children. When I picked the kids up that fateful night, as they walked across the street to my car, I heard him say, "I love you, and I'll see you tomorrow." It was reassuring to hear. As part of the custody agreement, he took the kids on Thursdays. Tomorrow was Thursday. We were finally getting back on track. It's funny what we find meaning in. For me, it was that phone call and that day of the week. It was the words, "I'll see you tomorrow." He waved to me and smiled. Relief. That was the man I recognized, and it was the last time I ever saw him.

I'm grateful that is my last image of him. We had a seventeen-year relationship. He was the love of my life, my best friend, husband, and father of our children. He was embedded in my life, even while divorced. When he didn't call the next day to confirm he was picking up the kids, I chalked it up to traffic. He had a long commute. He would show up. He always showed up for his kids. My son and I drove home in silence that afternoon. I could tell he was disappointed. The second call came as we were getting ready to pick up his little brother. It was Tom's best friend.

"He's gone," he said.

"What?" I asked.

"He's gone. He's dead."

I remember losing my breath. I thought I was going to pass out. My mind was spinning in disbelief. When I heard the distress in his voice, I had set the keys on the kitchen counter and walked into the bedroom, closing the door, leaving my son watching TV in the living room. I was trying to catch my breath. It felt like someone was gripping my rib cage, suffocating me. Things seemed to be moving in slow motion. Sunlight was streaming very slowly through the window onto the bedspread. I sat there staring at white flowers with a brown outline. Blue leaves. Soft colors reflecting the light coming in from the window. It was so quiet. I remember silence. And then the sound of my sobbing. Disbelief then confusion then questions. Lots of questions. His friend was asking the same questions over and over, blaming himself.

"He had been dead for a while," he said. "His body was cold."

It took me a while before I figured out that I was Tom's last phone call in those early morning hours. He had called me at 1:30 a.m., hung up the phone, and then killed himself. He was passing as I was waking up. We had been saying goodbye in person and in spirit.

Tom always had loyal friends. That day was no different. When the children and I had moved out, his best friend moved in to offer support. His friend blamed himself, angry that he had left him alone, angry that he didn't come home sooner that day, angry at Tom, angry at us for divorcing. He, like my parents, didn't want us to divorce. At that time, no one knew what was going on in the marriage, and no one knew about the addiction. For me, as a wife and mother, the addiction was something workable, as was the depression. I could have stayed. It would have been hard, but with my training as a counselor, those things felt manageable. The aggression and threats of violence were instant deal breakers. I just couldn't go down that road and put the children at risk.

Leaving my husband was the toughest decision I have ever had to make. For a woman to have to choose between protecting her children and standing by her husband, every outcome felt like a betrayal. In the world I was raised in, you didn't get divorced. You stood by your husband no matter what, and you kept the family together. You took care of your business privately, behind closed doors. Things like this didn't happen. The decisions I had to make were heart-wrenching. I was betraying all of it to leave the marriage and my husband for the safety of my children. I stand by that decision to this day. And there was a huge cost. "I'm sorry," was all I could say to our family friend that day. His friend, like so many people, would struggle with this loss too. They had been friends for over twenty-five years. What a loss for him.

The first time I saw great anger in a man was when my father lost his best friend of fifty years in a tragedy. I was fifteen. In all the years I had known my father, I think I had seen my him angry twice. The father I knew was such a solid, strong, and a stoically calm soul. He was in the living room, hysterical and sobbing. When he learned his friend had died, he started yelling at the top of his lungs. I could hear my mother's soft voice soothing him. There was so much agony in my father's voice. And such a sadness for him to lose such a long loyal and dear friend. In Brene Brown's book Braving the Wilderness: The Quest for True Belonging and the Courage to Stand Alone, she recounts stories about WWI veterans returning home and how some could be heard letting out a holler, a wail that would come out of a man who was suffering and full of agony. I recognized it that day with my father.

Now talking to my husband's best friend, I could hear it again, a similar loss for a man who was such a loyal and dear friend to my husband and our family for so many years. His holler was quiet yet still there, bearing the weight of a deep agony within his soul, from an unbelievable and unexpected tragedy. My memory dictated that sometimes men rage when they lose someone they love. His anger was familiar to me. He was just expressing it differently. He didn't yell; he didn't rage. He stayed and helped our family and then disappeared from our lives to recover in his own way. To learn how to live life now without his lifelong friend and to live instead with these terrible memories.

We are all left with little, as friends or family, as clinicians or scientists: only last bits of conversation; memories of perfectly normal and now suspect behaviors: an occasional note or journal entry, recollections of our own dealings with the dead, fragments we distort through guilt or anger or terrible loss.

—Kay Redfield Jameson
Night Falls Fast, Understanding Suicide

CHAPTER 2

LOSS BY SUICIDE

One of the most difficult things about dealing with suicide, like other tragedies, is that you are forced to say goodbye and let go of someone you love, often with no warning. It is sudden, shocking, and painful. You have no say, no opinion, no choice. You are asked to let go whether you want to or not. Unexpected and devastated, you are left behind, wondering what happened. There are no calendar notification, no email to give you a heads-up, no doctor's appointments with a future dismal medical prognosis. There may be indicators—talk about death, previous attempts, struggles with depression, and so on—but even with signs like that, you still don't know if it will ever happen. Unknowns leave the possibility of hope that death will not come. Hope that the person will at least keep living through the difficulties, that he or she will stay alive.

The shock factor of a suicide makes the loss that much more real and horrifying. It's a terrible reality to discover. Regrets make it difficult to accept what has happened; what-ifs fill your mind. There's guilt, there's doubt, there's confusion. You take inventory of all the things you could have done, should have said, changes that you could have made to elicit a different outcome. And rescue fantasies abound. Some scenario must be created in your mind to prove to yourself that you could have prevented the tragedy. Somehow you could have created a different outcome.

In her book *Trauma and Recovery, the Aftermath of Violence*, Judith Herman acknowledges that trauma occurs on two levels—exposure to the violence and exposure to the death. We have learned that trauma changes the traditional grief process that many experience. In her book *On Death and Dying*, Elisabeth

Kübler-Ross outlined five stages of grief: "The five stages—denial, anger, bargaining, depression, and acceptance—are the part of the framework that makes up our learning to live with the one we lost."

Kübler Ross's model was landmark work and has been the model counselors and professionals have used for decades. What we have learned more recently, however, is that a person grieving the loss of a loved one from suicide may not experience these five stages as someone who lost a loved one under different circumstances. Theirs is also an emotional response to the violence of suicide, to the way they died. We now know that losses like suicide often lead to what we now call complicated grief. It's complicated because it has many layers to it, making the grieving process and the healing sometimes longer and sometimes filled with more questions and confusion. It's like we are suddenly on a scaffold, climbing through the grief, seeking to better understand what happened, and to make sense of something.

Dr. Alan Wolfelt is an accomplished author in this realm. In his book *Understanding Your Suicide Grief: Ten Essential Touchstones for Finding Hope and Healing Your Heart*, he offers a different yet sound model for those grieving a loss such as this. The journey includes the need to open yourself up to the loss and the need to mourn. He suggests reaching out for help and exploring feelings that come up around the loss. Calling it a "transformative process," he also acknowledges the complicated nature of this type of grieving. Often there is a need for reconciliation. Carla Fine, the author of several books about suicide and loss, writes in her book *No Time to Say Goodbye, Surviving the Suicide of a Loved One* that many experiences can happen, including feelings of guilt and dealing with the "publicness" of suicide and the process of forgiveness. I found both authors' works very helpful in discovering how complex the grief from suicide loss can be.

The Alliance of Hope is a community created for those who lost someone to suicide. Among the many sources of support and information they offer, they also suggest a series of stages for grief. The stages address the process that evolves from the shocking, tragic loss of a loved one. I found their website as I was finishing this book, and I have to say that their grief stages were similar to my experience, something I found very consoling.

They suggest the process starts with *shock* and then *impact* as the reality hits about what has just happened. That is followed by what they call a *second crisis*, like a reliving of the trauma and its impact. Following this is a period of observation, followed by a turn or *shift in perspective and understanding*. Then a process of *reconstruction* begins. I refer to this as rewriting the family narrative, the storytelling we do after the tragedy. While we learn how to do this, they suggest working through various parts of the tragedy. This can help lead a person to a place of *integration*, a putting together of things in a way that makes sense and in a way that we can live with. This new narrative becomes integrated with the stories of our lives.

Suicide is a unique form of death in the sense that someone you loved sought this outcome. It's hard to be in denial about something so blatantly obvious. For many left behind, it is still an unfathomable perspective. Suicide of a loved one is a very unbelievable thing. Though not true for everyone, shock often takes the places of denial, guilt, confusion, and resignation take the place of acceptance. And with suicide, there is an unexpected burden placed on those left behind, those who were in relationship with the suicide victim, all sharing a different perspective, need, or wish left unfulfilled by this unexpected tragedy, wondering what they could have done to prevent it.

Most humans do not wish ill on their loved ones. Usually, it's quite the opposite. We want our loved ones to know we are there no matter what, and we love them. We want to help, offer support, and champion them. Even if love can't change circumstances, the love and support offered by others can be incredibly healing in getting through difficult times, whether in our minds or in our lives. As loved ones, we often want to have a chance to offer that because we value their life. And we need them.

I loved Tom. That has been one of the hardest parts of this process for me. I still love him. He was my husband for many years. He filled a big part of my life. I planned on him being in my life and our children's lives for many years. It has been hard to let him go. That's not denial but fact. I feel this way partially because his death happened when it shouldn't have. He was at the peak of his life and his career, launching into the echelons of success, success he had worked *towards* for decades. He deserved the happiness that comes with that and the satisfaction of seeing all the work he did pay off. He had so much at his fingertips.

It came at a bad time also because we were nurturing and growing our family, something we had worked at together for a long time. This needed to happen whether we were married or not. The nurturing was still needed. We were a unit with two children incredibly dependent on us. It came at a bad time partially because of our divorce. I wanted a chance for us to become friends and heal the wounds that had been created. We needed time and a chance to create a new chapter for our family, a new way to coexist. I may have been angry with him at times, disappointed or frustrated, but I never would have wished him ill or for him to die.

Because he chose suicide, he left a lot of unfinished business in our relationship. I have carried it with me for years, willingly. The cycle in my mind goes something like this: events that happened, what

I could have done differently, how things would have played out differently, and how those different choices would have led to him still being alive today. End result: he'd still be with us. With, perhaps, a better ending.

And then futility of knowing we'll never see him again hits. We'll never hear his voice, see his smile, hear his laugh, share moments again, feel his thriving, his vitality. They say you never get over the loss of a loved one's suicide but have to learn how to live with it. Even divorced, he filled a big space in my life as a partner for so many years, as a co-parent in our family unit, and as a co-provider for the family. As sole parent, I carry the burden of the loss now, with the understanding of the impact it has and will continue to have on our family.

One of the distinct features of suicide is that it leaves this agony in its wake because it is not a natural event. In some ways, the suicide is the first holler, the first agony of the spirit. It's a wail that doesn't get answered, and then it elicits wails from those left behind. It's an interruption; better yet, it is a disruption of life and relationship. It creates a trauma that opens a new timeline of events that follow, subsequent by-products of the suicide. It ends up being an event of catastrophic proportions that connects every aspect of your life and then changes the direction of your life, whether you want it to or not. Things you thought you could expect and plan for are suddenly gone and replaced with this new life and events you had no idea even existed.

I remember standing in the living room, waiting for the coroner to arrive. And just the thought of that was shocking. Standing in the living room in our house, waiting for a coroner, didn't feel real. I was standing there crying and waiting, not sure what to do next, watching police officers and paramedics pass through the front door of our home. I remember thinking, *We are too young to have a coroner in our home. How could this be happening now?*

I spoke briefly to the police and then made my way to the backyard as the coroner and paramedics brought his body down the stairs. It was the only place I could get a small bit of privacy. The first call I made was to my sister and brother-in-law, who jumped in the car to come up. The next call was to his sister in Florida. That was an awful conversation. She was heartbroken, and I was the conduit giving her the bad news, like I had to for many. My ex-husband may have been alone when he died, but he was not alone in his life. I had a lot of calls to make. And they would all be painful.

Through my tears, I saw them struggling to carry the gurney with his covered body down that set of stairs that had a sharp right angle at the bottom. It was not an easy staircase to maneuver. We had many conversations over the years about how steep those stairs were. We kept one of the dogs off them because he was so clumsy, we were sure he'd go tumbling down them one day. The baby gates were up for years. We had never been presented with the difficult task of someone having to carry a body down them. Suddenly, it wasn't our family room anymore. It was now an empty house with the owner deceased. And I was outside looking in, like I had felt during those final years of our marriage.

After his body had been taken out, the coroner asked to sit with me at kitchen table. The house was quiet, the paramedics were gone, and the policemen were starting to dissipate. The familiar kitchen light lit the kitchen table, the table where we shared so many meals. As the coroner spoke, I could feel him watching me, checking my state of mind, gauging how much information he should give me in that moment, and seeing how he could help. He was pragmatic and compassionate. He had a difficult role to play, that of sharing an intimate experience with strangers. I admired him. He was present and compassionate, yet emotionally reserved. Practical and logistical, while connecting with loved ones to inform, educate, and assist in the middle of a tragedy. He informed me about the inquiry, including the autopsy, and the burial that would follow. Decisions would have to be made. The morgue was backed up. It would take a while before his report was completed and the body could be released. The setting of expectations. It didn't matter in this case. This was not the event to me. The major event had already transpired; he had already died. That was the big-ticket item. From here on out, these were just tasks, getting ready for the next stage of this new death process I was being forced into.

The coroner made the same comment several times, as if to embed it in my brain, "Suicide is a selfish act." Not compassionate, but pragmatic. He was trying to offer a different perspective. A realistic one, one of fact. He'd make a comment about why people suicide and how difficult it was for those left behind. Then he sat and waited patiently as I cried and tried to take in what he said. To be honest, it didn't matter to me how selfish it was. There was an agony created that day that would never be truly healed. Agony and shock overrode all logic and rational. He was gone. Something terrible had just happened.

My mind was focused on how I was going to tell our children they would never see their father again. I wondered how they would react. They, of course, would be unable to fully fathom the impact it would have on their lives. We had been forced into a loss we didn't want or need. Tom didn't need to be dead. He didn't need to suicide. What he needed was to get clean and sober. He needed to get his health and his mind back. The Tom I knew was one of the smartest men I ever met. He needed to reestablish a healthy parenting relationship with his kids. He needed it, and they needed it. And then he needed to reconcile with me. But even that didn't need to happen. His health and wellness, his state of mind, his survival as a human being needed to happen first and foremost. His staying alive was paramount in importance. Instead, none of it happened. There was an abrupt ending to an unfinished life and story. Unfair and unnecessary. And who said I had to accept this? Perhaps he was not the only person who was acting selfishly.

If we learn to open our own hearts, anyone, including the people who drive us crazy, can be our teacher.

—Pema Chodron

CHAPTER 3

TIED TOGETHER THROUGH LOVE

Death, with all the suffering and negativity, also brings closure. A real ending. This short, unsettled chapter in our lives abruptly closed the day he died. The stress, addiction issues, and ongoing problems that developed over the past couple years were suddenly over. I figured that because of the conflict between us at the time, grief would take a brief hold in my life and then dissipate. I thought I would help the kids deal with their loss, and then we would all move on. Happily, move on and just put this mess of a situation behind us. Initially, I was ready to pack it all away.

Instead, something else happened. Much to my surprise, the grief continued through the first year. It turned out that losing the love of my life was something I would need to be with. But then the grieving continued well beyond that first year. And instead of getting over it, I had to develop a relationship with loss to get a better understanding of what was happening inside me. In Buddhism they say, "push nothing away." So, I surrendered to it. In fact, I invited it in.

I found myself going back in time during my meditations, reviewing events that happened over the years. It was a review all our years of living together. There was meaning there; I just had to find it. I didn't know it at the time, but I was starting a journey that would take years. There is a famous Rumi quote, "You have to keep breaking your heart until it opens." I had not realized how closed my heart had become during the process of separation and divorce. I had shut down a part of myself to get through the process. I had to remember what it was like to feel deep sadness and then contend with a new player—suffering—as I began to really understand what happened to Tom. I had to learn to be fully present with the grief, the immensity of this loss, and all the complicated feelings that come with losing a loved one to suicide. I also had to let go of the future I had secured in my mind and the life I saw us both having, which were not going to happen now. The plans we had made in the years to come for him to be with his children. Suffering also appeared at times as a state of unrelenting misery, something I was not familiar with. It shows up when you have the poignant realization that the person you loved actively chose to kill himself and leave you. It hits when you realize that not only did, they abruptly leave, they killed themself in a violent and angry way, in an angry, unresolved hurtful kind of way. In a way you could not have imagined. In a way that you would never wish on another human soul. It's at that moment you feel and carry the burden of their states of mind and the levels of misery they carried. It's agonizing, and it's miserable. Deep empathy is carried in the heart. And there I was, now experiencing it. I was learning how deeply unhappy he was.

Authors Brook Noel and Pamela Blair wrote, "Women are more apt to see relationship as the central point in their life. Often women's relationships and emotional ties to children and spouse come before any other priority, including self-care." As I began to feel the depth of this loss, I also realized that I was the last surviving parent in our family system. And I was carrying the loss of more than just my ex-husband. It was also the loss of the father of two children who adored and needed him. It was the loss of a seventeen-year relationship. It was the loss of my best friend and husband for so many years. It was the loss of our marriage. It was the shock and loss within our community of friends and family. This relationship, this man, and the roles we played, had been a central point in my life, in divorce, and were now in death.

There was also confusion that can arise about why a person committed suicide. It's the slow realization of the impact that act has on so many people. It's the statement suicide makes, letting others know how much suffering the person was going through when he or she died. And it included all the questions about where one's soul goes after committing suicide. I went to enough masses, had read the Bible, and had attended classes about religion to know that suicide was not, by any means, a good thing. That act supposedly sent you to either limbo or hell, Dante's *Inferno* or beyond. Both are places you don't want to end up. Wonderings about existence and the afterlife filled my mind. And not just mine, but our children's minds too. One day our oldest son asked, "How could a God allow something like this to happen?" That was the moment our oldest son stopped believing in God. I had a lot of questions to answer. So began my journey of breaking my heart back open and gaining a more solid understanding of myself and the world around me.

My first big insight came on a day when I was praying. As my mind started to drift and shift into memories of Tom and I together, I felt this warmth suddenly fill my soul. I found a feeling of love slowly pushing its way up, up through the years of marriage and layers of memories, to the surface. A warmness that would fill my soul permanently as I remembered so many good things and how much we had loved each other. I had forgotten how much I loved Tom. Love had been forgotten and was now needing to be remembered. It was asking for a seat at the table.

This caught me by surprise. In some ways, it was like coming home again to myself. The grief was slowly moving its way through my soul, uncovering layers of history, sifting through memories of the lives we had lived together, moment after moment; our narratives of living as a family and the lives we created that were being weaved together. From the moment we met, we were very much in love. It was good, healthy love. It was without addiction rearing its ugly head, without anger, hostility, or conflict. The grief was making connections in my mind, and that's when my grieving started to make more sense. I was starting to remember what things used to be like. Slowly I felt the love that we had. During all we had been through, I had forgotten that we had once been a very happy and healthy family.

For most of those years, Tom and I had been in love, deeply passionate love. In Christianity the term agape love refers to God's unconditional and ever-present love, desire and need. More than the lust of the heart or need for companionship. That was what brought us and kept us together. We had been so deeply in love and so committed to that love for many years. I suddenly found myself remembering so many good things with so much love in them. A new narrative began to form that included the real love and the need to remember the good things because there were so many good things to remember. It was not about denying the bad things that happened or idolizing him (that was definitely not happening.) Rather, it was about learning to be OK with everything that happened and then digging deep to pull up of the roots of our relationship, to return to where we started, which, in this case, with Agape love. We fell in love weeks after we met. I had loved this man raucously, madly, divinely for many years. And he had loved me. That I was sure of. That was our foundation. We had had a passionate love affair that lasted through most of our marriage. Our souls were tied together through love. And that love was still there, deep in my soul. I needed to acknowledge it, honor it, and accept it. And I'm guessing he did too. As Sarah Bareilles would say, I had to put, "my heart at the wheel." Our love had to become a part of my narrative, whether I wanted it to or not. I began to see that love, loss, and grief were so intertwined in my process, and love needed to be acknowledged for me to heal. It would also be needed to heal our family.

After months of sitting with all this, I started to find our love again. And it has helped me immensely. This doesn't mean the suicide was reconciled or the problems that led to divorce didn't exist. It doesn't take away the agony of losing him. But it's a reminder that love was the thread that weaved our existences together. Most of my memories were ones of happiness, love, and peace. They were of our family, our time together, of us supporting each other. I discovered it would be impossible for me ever to hate him. If I was going to be honest, I could be angry with him, I could feel disappointed and hurt, but I could never hate him because I still loved him. Realizing this was a breakthrough for me. I still loved the man I married and was with for so many years. That man was also who Tom really was, not that mess of an addict that he had become. With my heart at the wheel, this would be the road we would take to help our family heal. Love played a critical role in our relationship, and now it needed to take its rightful place in the narrative. I was reminded how powerful a force it is and that it is manifested in our hearts, our minds, and our souls. It can also guide healing.

I can now say that I loved that man, even in his worst state. My denial was not that he died or that he was gone but that I didn't want to love him anymore, even though I still did. I didn't want to love that horrible man who had become a miserable, angry addict. Being with someone or choosing to stay in a relationship with a person is not the same as loving someone. Love doesn't pick people based on geographic location, the good or the bad they do, whether their name is on the marriage certificate, or whether you live under the same roof. Pure love, the Agape love, transcends all of that.

This is not to say I don't struggle with forgiveness. It's still a hard story to tell. It doesn't take away my children's pain. My logical brain says I should not have loved him; I should have cut him off and forgotten him. I get it. But we forget that we really live in the gray area of life. We idolize relationships we see others having, filling in the blank spaces with our own idealism and projections. Or we watch unrealistic conversations in movies between characters that don't even exist. The reality is that most relationships and love are messy. And it's not always a clear-cut decision. Things aren't always logical. Love is complicated, life is complicated, divorce and death are complicated. This story is not black or white. Nor is grief. There is no linear process here. There are days even years later, as I write this, that I struggle with the loss some days and anger or disappointment others. Sometimes I still feel the frustration about certain things that happened. Some days I am filled with great stories and warm memories. There are moments when I hear us laughing as I relay to our children funny stories about their father. I know we all still feel the void of where he should be. That never goes away.

My heart also feels sad when I think about him. I feel sad about the unfinished business in his life and in our relationship. I feel sad about his unmet potential. I feel sad about the relationships he is missing with his children, all the things he has to witness from afar now. I feel especially sad for our children, for their broken hearts and all the moments they will miss with him. And I see that they are aware of that, too, and it makes it that much worse. I am so aware of the void created the day he suicided, especially when I look at our beautiful boys. To sit with this kind of loss, real deep loss, is hard to do. You must be willing to break open your heart and really hear what your soul needs.

I am most surprised at the power of our love. Our love was our story of togetherness. It's the reason our children exist, why we had such a long history together. It's a part of our narrative in this life that doesn't have to be forgotten because he became an addict and then suicided. I've spent these years since his death learning how to tell our story and how to weave such a tragedy into our family narrative. How to fill some of that empty space with love. It's still a work in progress, maybe not a happy ending, but one that I can live with as we move forward without him.

You will lose someone you can't live without, and your heart will be badly broken, and the bad news is that you never completely get over the loss of your beloved. But this is also the good news. They live forever in your broken heart that doesn't seal back up. And you come through it.

—Anne Lamott

CHAPTER 4

UNSETTLE MY GROUND

Today I am driving down to the South Bay to attend an education fair. Being an extroverted salesperson is not my wheelhouse, but I need clients, so I do it. I am reminded daily of his passing, mostly by the children. We are dealing with the loss as best as we can.

As I drive through Marin County and pass the familiar views and exits, I am reminded of how Tom and I met, how we shared our first kiss in the bank parking lot off the freeway, how we moved down to the peninsula, got married, bought a home, and started our family. So many drives over the Golden Gate Bridge, listening to Diana Krall, and talking. So much to say to each other. So much time spent together. Driving over the bridge, I realize that I have not made this drive since his death. I drive through the Presidio in San Francisco, look at the off ramps and remembering the Starbucks off 19th Avenue, where he'd double-park to run in for coffee. Double-parking on a busy street in San Francisco, such a city thing. And that day we made an impromptu stop on Union Street on the way home to see a movie. *You've Got Mail* was our first movie together. I couldn't believe he wanted to see a chick flick. That was when I learned he was such a romantic. Lucky me. We laughed at the same moments in the movie, as I realized I was sitting next to my future husband.

I flash back to years later, when we took the kids to Fisherman's Wharf to see the submarine. The seals happily sitting on the docks at Pier 39, barking and jumping in and out of the water. Fighting hordes of people so we could eat at Alioto's, near the water. San Francisco held a lot of fun memories for us. It was an integral part of our life together.

Merging onto 280, heading into San Mateo County, I see the water glistening on the reservoir. This route, for a while, was our drive on the weekends, heading back and forth to Marin to see the family congregated at my sister's house. I didn't expect so many reminders today. The smell of his cologne as we passed the Highway 92 off ramp, Yanni symphonies floating through the car, Tom's phone always ringing. The debates we had about having the top up or down. We loved convertibles and hated them, especially when the top started to leak. The restaurant parking lot in Burlingame where he proposed, of all nights, the night I had a splitting headache. I had no idea he was proposing. So many memories. Laughing together, crying, happy, excited, sitting in the car looking at the engagement ring. Sitting in that convertible that had started to leak. That night it didn't matter.

Over the past few years since his passing, I have shed many tears. More than I thought I had. There is something so unsettling about suicide. There is a sadness that lingers with this feeling of so much unfinished business. And it's a terrible way to die. Most who die by suicide die alone and often in violent and painful ways. The truth is that the shadow of his death has haunted me, filling me with so many regrets, so many things I would have done differently. And so much guilt. Things I would say that I never did, choices I would make to have different outcomes.

I want to write a different ending to this story. I want a second take or a do-over. I want this ending to be an outtake, the one they were going to use but decided not to. Too dark, too sad. No love or happiness. Nope, can't use it. Find a better ending. Audiences won't like it. I don't like it. It's painful and ugly. In my happy ending, he gets clean and sober. He admits to the addiction and asks for help. He decides he wants to live. Choosing to stay alive would be the climax of the film, where the symphony plays the loudest, and the audience cheers. Yes, my ending would have someone who wants to fight for his life. Hang on to it. Value life. Stay alive. Fight. Survive and stay with us.

Then he would start to become himself again, only a better version, resolved, healthy, and determined to stay on this earth—in this life—with us for as long as possible. We would start to rebuild our friendship. And I would get to tell him all the things I missed saying, like, "I'm sorry," "You matter," "You are loved," "You are valued and appreciated," "You are irreplaceable." In time, he would start to feel the value of his existence, his value in our lives, and to really understand our need for him. He would put us first again. We would all move forward together. Our marriage might not survive in this scenario, but we would work as friends for many years and as co-parents to raise our children together. Our children would receive the family, love, peace, and support they deserve. Instead, I am here today driving alone down a familiar highway I had forgotten about. One that caught me by surprise.

By the time I get to San Jose, I am crying and drained. Not a great way to start an all-day event. I'm reminded that grief can take you by surprise and level your emotional landscape. It just empties you. I want to be alone with my grief now. Instead, I must go talk to people.

Great.

I look around and see I must have taken a wrong turn. So now I'm lost too. Lost in San Jose. Perfect. When we bought our first home here, Tom always drove. He never got lost. I should have paid more attention. There are a lot of things I should have paid more attention to. As I pull into the parking lot of the shopping mall, I realize that I came in a different way. I recognize the parking lot and see I'm in a mall that Tom and I used to come to. The first time I traveled with him for work, this mall was one of the malls where he had to set up kiosks for Pac-Bell. I remember sitting in the car, waiting for him and thinking how boring his work must be. I was struck by how much he loved it.

As I park the car, I realize I am directly in front of the restaurant he took me to for our twelfth anniversary. We sat in the car talking about how many good years of marriage we had. Then a couple rough ones hit us. We laughed about it, happy and determined to move past that period together. We were seeing a counselor, and things had gotten much better.

A strange thought hits me: *The restaurant has outlived my ex-husband and our marriage.* A sobering thought. Death does that. You think weird thoughts sometimes. It's been years since we were here, yet everything looks the same—the trees, the buildings, the cars, and all the people. Except he is missing. His energy, physical presence, and spirit are gone. Everything else is moving forward without him. It's as if he were never here.

But he was, with me, living our life together. I park the car and sit there for a minute, taking in the front view of the restaurant. Instead of being with me today, he is just a memory. A painful one. I always assumed he'd be around. He'd be nearby. And he's not.

As I make my way through the parking lot, I am reminded that I don't like groups of people. I was the introvert, and he was the extroverted sales guy. For years everyone loved Tom. He could walk into a room and light it up. Like my mother, people loved him. They were drawn to his smile and to his enthusiasm and friendliness. He was naturally engaging. Until the addiction hit, I was always so proud to have him as my husband and the father of our children. I was happy to stand next to him, proud to introduce him as my partner. I was always so impressed with the work he did, of the kind of human being he was, the father he was, the way his values aligned with his personality. Tom was one of the best things that ever happened to me.

The man I knew and married would have been excited for me to head out and attend an event for my new business. He would have wanted to come with me and sell the hell out of my products and services. It was second nature to him. He would have been all in. His enthusiasm was always so contagious. I realize as I walk into the mall alone that I could have really used his expertise today. I am so out of my wheelhouse. But he is nowhere to be found. Alone, I make my way into the sea of people flooding the tables. This, like so many things now, I will have to face alone.

We always deceive ourselves twice about the people we love-first to their advantage, then to their disadvantage.

—Albert Camus

CHAPTER 5

SOMETHING ESSENTIAL IS MISSING

The process of grieving a loved one's suicide is difficult terrain to cover. In the documentary *Grief Walker*, Stephen Jenkinson said, "Something essential is missing," meaning the need in society to talk about death, the need to build a language around the experiences of living and dying. In this case, I would say what was essential in our little part of the world was the loss of a father, a primary component of our family system. Suddenly, he was missing. The essentialness of his existence was gone. I found I could rarely talk about it with others. It wasn't because people didn't want to talk about it. Maybe there was some of that, but mostly because a deep loss like this is hard in general to talk about. It can be socially awkward talking about something so deeply personal with people you know as acquaintances. It just doesn't always feel right. Suicide is also a difficult subject in general because it's not just about death. It's about living, about why we are here, our purposes for being. A death by suicide brings up so much, and it often feels like an elephant in the room. I've had this elephant traveling with me for years now.

When someone you love commits suicide, each discovery in this process feels like rocks you must climb over. One difficult topic is the suicide itself. For more traditionally conservative religious communities, blame and judgment can be attached to someone's suicide. Suddenly judgement is introduced into the death process, as if the death weren't difficult already. The belief that a loved one is going to hell or limbo because he or she suicided is probably one of the most damaging and hurtful things someone could say to a grieving individual, let alone think. The fact of the matter is that we really don't know where a soul goes when someone suicides. If God truly knows every hair on person's head, every essence of their being, and loves with Agape love, why would he abandon them at the most critical time for that soul? It would make more sense if God took their soul and helped heal them, brought them to the inner sanctum of love and forgiveness. It seems that compassion and love are better fillers here instead of hurtful dialogue. Sometimes it's also better to just sit with someone and not say anything.

What also makes it hard to talk about is the fact that suicide scares people. That is often where the judgement comes, sometimes masked in religious righteousness. The act of taking one's life is a direct reminder that we have the power to extinguish ourselves. It's a blatant reminder that we live, and then we die. That we live on an existential plane of not knowing what happens to us when we die or even understanding why we are here.

Possible judgment, guilt, and confusion sit on one side of you as the family member left behind, while the insidious nature of someone planning his or her suicide sits on the other, making this ugly terrain. Wondering why a loved one did it, those left behind sometimes also have the horrific realization that it was carefully thought out. A sobering fact about suicide is that it was, though not always, planned. Preparations were made to align with some obscure grisly outcome that makes no sense. Then he or she executes the plan, and in this case, dies. The individual actively seeks to kill himself or herself. Or as Carl Jung might say, kill the Self. The symbolism in this case, as Jung wrote, "implies something vague, unknown and hidden from us." Killing, in this case, one's essentialness. Reflection of this process is brutal and ugly, reminding those of us left behind that terrible things can happen to our loved ones. And that we didn't protect them. How could we?

They say when someone decides to die, they reach a calmness, a sense of resolve. In psychiatry, they have a term coined by Victor Frankl: the "delusion of the reprieve." When a man is about to be executed, he gets a brief glimmer of hope that somehow his execution might get a stay. Beyond all odds, he'll somehow be spared. When a suicidal person decides to go through with it, there is, in a sense, a sort of delusion of reprieve. In a twisted way, the individual has been given a perceived way out.

With suicide, the paradox is a complex one. The person has surrendered to the idea of dying but presents the exact opposite to the rest of the world, reflecting the internal battle he or she has been having about living and dying. Perhaps they have their own fantasies, hoping before they die that whatever is tormenting them will stop. That something will abruptly change. Or maybe it is in the understanding that because someone is ending his or her life, the torment will also end. A wishful type of reprieve. The paradox is that to the rest of the world, they show the desire to live again, even though they have made the decision to take their life. The decision to die becomes a great act in this drama, bringing a peace of mind, so to speak. But in reality, the will and the soul have been surrendered and sacrificed. The offering of a life has been made. The delusion is that routines and behaviors return, and the outlook temporarily becomes one of wanting to live. Temporary in their mind because they know it will end soon. It's a futile, false, and brief presentation.

And it fools many of us. The days leading up to his death showed Tom resolute on the outside. He looked and sounded like he was finally ready to move on after a rough few years. Even the conversation with his best friend the night before reflected a willingness to turn a corner and start a new chapter in his life. That same evening, as the kids were leaving the house, he had said to them, "I love you, and I'll see you tomorrow." I had recognized that person, and it felt so good to see him again. I was glad to see him back.

But in reality, he was playing out his last refrain. The last line in this play was to say goodbye in a hopeful, positive way. In a hopeful and *deceitful* way. Dr. Yalom said, "Every person must choose how much truth he can stand." In those final moments of seeing his children, Tom's truth was entirely somewhere else, locked in the recesses of his mind. It turned out he had no intention of seeing them the next day. That was the last time we ever saw him, and that has been one bitter pill for me to swallow. Those moments now, when I reflect on my truth, felt like such a betrayal.

He timed his death to occur amid a series of changes: the divorce papers were signed, the house sold, he landed a new job, and just days after he regained custody with a court order mandating a sobriety program and anger management class. Tom was reflecting forward movement to look like he was taking care of things. But inside, the opposite was happening; he was preparing to leave. He was getting ready to abandon all of it. And all of us. His resolution was to die. Deep inside, I suspect he was raging mad. Another paradox with a false presentation.

He set things up to finish the whole divorce process in a way so everyone would know he really wasn't happy with the outcomes. And he wasn't going to put up with any of it. He left it so we would never be able to reconcile or co-parent again. He also would never move out of the house or start a new job. And as for the addiction, that definitely wasn't going anywhere. It was clear from his actions that I was to be the one left to pick up the pieces of the remnants of our life together—from packing up our home to closing escrow to notifying family and friends of his death and organizing his funeral. It would be me left to feel the reverberations of his suicide on the communities of people surrounding us. I was the one assigned as the keeper of the family memories, good and bad. It would also be my responsibility to explain and support his legacy to our children. And somehow rewrite a legacy, one that no one ever expected. I would be left to reflect what had happened and all that would be missed, jammed into a time capsule.

I was also now to become the permanent sole parent raising our children. The forever parent. I was now responsible for all of it. More bitter pills to swallow. In some ways, it feels like because of the timing, his suicide was a *screw you* to me, the judge, and his loved ones, who all said he needed to get help and straighten his life out. He simply wasn't going to do it. The timing of all this has never escaped me. He was very angry when he died. He was in a blaming, hateful state. His suicide seems in some ways like the reflection of a battle cry.

I can't speak too much about his rage or frame of mind because it's his to own. But I can tell you that being on the receiving end of all this was painful and heartbreaking, to say the least. And this is one of the parts of this story that is difficult for me to reflect on. It is the pool that holds the waters of agony and regret. This ending felt like an epic failure for all of us. First fissures, then big cracks, and then a catastrophic break in the walls. Human beings thrive on living, success, and happiness. We overcome, we endure, and we move on. We also thrive on seeing those we care about OK, happy, and contented. We have an innate desire to support others. What happened to Tom was the complete opposite. And the state of mind it left in some others was equally terrible. We assume those left behind get over it and eventually move on. But not everyone does. And in this case, not everyone has. Sometimes things like this change people and not for the better. I have witnessed deep loss and unreconcilable anger in others. I have seen people disappear and relationships fall apart. I don't think he wished for any of that. Sometimes we simply can't foresee the true consequences of our actions.

I don't say this lightly, but if I had to look for a positive in all this, the only silver lining amid these sordid facts, the saving grace in all of this was that things immediately settled down for our sons. When he passed, their energy levels settled way down. They no longer had to wonder what was happening with their father. The fighting, anger, and worry, along with the stress of the divorce, were also laid to rest. Calmness sat at our feet for the first time in a long time. The children, still in shock, now had one solid, secure home. Overnight, they now had a regular routine and a responsible parent to rely on full time. Not a perfect parent, but 100 percent there for them. No more awkward conversations about the other parent; no more confusion about why they couldn't see their father. The divorce process was difficult in and of itself, but I didn't fully comprehend how stressful carrying the burden of an active addict around was.

For the first few months, things became calm. Their souls became very calm. I think on some level, they knew he was struggling. They had seen changes in his behavior and felt his pain and unsettledness. His death allowed those burdens to be lifted. For a long time, our eldest son would talk about how unhappy his dad was and how he had wanted to help him. Even at nine, he could feel something wasn't right. Years later, he would tell me how responsible he felt for his father.

The boys had a new task to attend to following their father's death: integrate the permanent absence of him. They had to come to terms with the fact that they would never see him again. As time started to pass, the boys and I started a regular routine in our home. It was a big adjustment for all of us. And there was an obvious absence of his presence in everyday life.

I adore our children, as did Tom. That was one thing I loved about him; he loved being a dad. He was also an integral part of my support system as a parent, especially when I felt like parenting was too intense. He was always there as backup, just around the corner. He obviously didn't know how much I needed him.

As the surviving parent, the boys naturally latched on to me after Tom died. In some ways, it was a primal response, a survival mechanism: food, clothing, shelter, emotional safety, and a secure attachment. Children need a secure attachment to feel safe. Perhaps Maslow had the wrong order. Perhaps securing emotional safety and the attachment come first, before food, clothing, and shelter. Harlow's monkeys proved that. These kids were now using one parent as the surrogate for the loss of the other. It can be terrifying for children when a parent dies. What I know is that those kids were calm, but they were also holding on for dear life. And I was their flotation device.

The wound is the place where the heart enters.

—Rumi

CHAPTER 6

THE REPLAY

At the time of Tom's death, I was working outside the home. When he passed, I was given four days of bereavement leave and then asked to return to my full-time position. This was as a single parent with two grieving boys. It was unbelievable, yet it had to happen that way. The world does not stop for death. Each day while driving, I found myself thinking first of the tasks that had to get taken care of on my never-ending to-do lists. Then my focus naturally and repeatedly turned back to his death.

Suicide is a tragedy that leaves an open forum for so many unanswered questions to be asked and explored. Our minds naturally try to make sense of things. Driving was one of the few times during my day when I was alone and could think freely. My mind instinctively went back to trying to make sense of it and to put an order to Tom's suicide. As morbid as this type of thinking and reliving sounds, it was actually a relief. I was "on" so much of the time, especially having to work helping others. I had to appear like I was OK and able to do my job. Friends and family were worried, so I put myself together as much as possible for them. My kids had a lot going on, so I focused on them as much as I could. Others were struggling with losing him, and in some way, I felt like I was taking care of others and their grief as much as my own. Driving in silence and thinking freely on the way to work each morning was a commodity I began to appreciate. It was a lifeline I desperately needed.

The drive each day was about thirty minutes. I developed the habit of rummaging through topics related to his death. It usually started with the morning of his death, that phone call I received at 1:30 a.m. The call I did not answer. Sometimes I spent the whole drive fantasizing about what it could have been like had I picked up the phone. I would play it out—keep him on the phone, throw some shoes and a jacket on, knock on the neighbors' door, ask them to watch the children, race over to the house, all while calling the police and paramedics. He would open the door, and I would wait with him on the porch. I would get to see him one more time. I would get to tell him all the things I never got to say—how important he was, how much he mattered, how sorry I was for my part in the divorce, how I wanted him to be OK, how important he was to the kids, and how he would never be better off being away from them. I would remind him how much his children and I loved and needed him.

Then I would ask him to fight, fight to get clean and sober, fight for a clean mind, fight for the kids' sakes, fight to simply stay alive. I would have had a chance to talk him into going to the hospital, assuring him I would be there as much as possible. I would have told him I would spend every cent on a detox program for his sobriety. I would have told him that I would be there in a way that I hadn't been before. I would have told him how much we needed him alive.

Sometimes during the drive I reviewed his death and that whole day, every event that happened, from beginning to end—the phone call at 1:30 a.m., getting up in the morning and not feeling right, heading to work and struggling to focus, leaving work early, getting my son's call, going back to the house, getting the call about Tom's death, coordinating things with friends to take care of the kids while I went over to the house, the police questioning me as I arrived, not being allowed to go upstairs to see his body, how I wanted to hug him even though he was dead, all the questions I had, how upset his best friend was, all the phone calls I had to make. And watching from the backyard as the coroner and paramedics brought the body down, his lifeless body all covered up. I would review the coroner's arrival, how the ambulance with the two paramedics waited patiently outside, how respectful the police officers were in the house that day, how much they had to coordinate and handle, how attentive they were, how they encouraged me not to see the body, and how they offered to help. I remember being acutely aware that as my ex-husband disappeared, other men, strong men, had taken his place in different ways ever so briefly over the months to help me in this new place I was in as a single mother, now a divorced widow.

Some of those men were standing in front of me that day, offering boundaries, advice, support, and to listen. Strong police officers, a coroner, my ex-husband's best friend, and my brother-in-law. I remembered the police would take turns interviewing me, keep me talking, gathering information. I would answer questions and then burst into tears. They would stop and patiently wait until I could continue. They offered to take the puppy we had found in the bathroom. They offered suggestions. They offered support as best they could. I will never forget that. On that day I learned many people express empathy and compassion through their actions.

And then the important task of how I would tell the children they would never see their father again would enter my mind. I remember sitting the boys down in our living room late that evening and holding them. I remember not knowing what to expect or what else to say. I remember the shock on their faces, as I worried about our children. They would be without their father for the rest of their lives. I remember feeling sorry for them and wondering how this happened. And feeling this huge gap in existence, like a black hole had just been created, and we were getting sucked in. All the details would pass through my mind, like an inventory, as I drove. From the night before until later that evening, when I told the children. I replayed it all in my mind, sorting, thinking, and contemplating. As I drove into the parking lot of my work, our children would fill my mind. So much loss. So much for our children to bear. Then I would pack it all up in my mind, put it away, head into work, and pretend like everything was OK. We all knew things weren't OK, but I went through the motions anyway because life doesn't stop for death.

I don't like the anger, but I'm feeling a lot of it lately. I wonder "why?" more and more. "Why them?" "Why now?" "Why this?" "Why us?" "Why this way?" "Why?" All I get in return is silence. No answer. I'm more irritable and edgy. My fuse is shorter. I don't like this. I don't like being angry, but I am.

—Gary Roe, *Grief Walk*

CHAPTER 7

THE ANGER THAT FOLLOWS SUICIDE

The calm in our house lasted a few months. Then the kids started acting out as the anger of losing their father reared its ugly head. The anger was not directed at me but at the world around them. Fights and disruptive behaviors became regular events at school. Opposition, anger, or defiance became the new norm. I parented, I soothed, I disciplined. The teachers, principals, and I met more regularly. The kids acted out in waves and then things settled. It usually ramped up during the holidays.

Actually, holidays brought the fighting like clockwork. I began to hate the Fourth of July, which was, of course, Tom's favorite holiday. I was a 24/7 parent, flying solo. Something I never planned. We came into our marriage with a lot of expectations for each other, including that we would stay married. Tom and I had married for the long haul. We made plans. We planned our future together. We planned to raise our family and grow old together. We used to talk about getting old together, sitting on the porch in our rocking chairs, watching the sunset. Him not being in the picture was never part of the plan. Never even an inkling. Now here I was, going this alone. And I hated it.

The first year following his death turned out to be the time to deal with the aftermath from the tsunami that hit us. In addition to all the emotion turmoil we were going through, I worked a fifty-hour week. The kids were gone from 7 a.m. until 6 p.m. weekdays. Days were long. We were often tired. They did the best they could to help me out. I filled our weekends at church, soccer practice, with long games on the weekends or playdates with friends. We hung out regularly with family.

Parenting was intensive, as was living, as I slowly sacrificed my personal life to be with them. Our family had taken a hit. Those boys were worth going the extra mile. I became aware of our living together, in unison, every day. Underneath was a desire to stay on top of it because the loss was so hard on us. What you don't hear about is what happens to the loved ones after a person suicides. You see the story in the news or hear about it from someone, with a brief mention about who was left behind. And then nothing. This is what happens. Survival. Survival after the devastation.

I desperately wanted us to survive. I didn't want us to fail. And I didn't just want to *survive*; I wanted them, all of us, to *thrive* again. The boys initially didn't know their father suicided. It was something I waited to tell them. It just seemed like too much for their young minds to deal with. I wanted them to have time—time to heal, time to choose being alive after the grief. I wanted them to have time so I could show them and teach them that their lives mattered, that the world needed them. I needed them. I wanted to hear their laughter again. So I gave them time to regain feelings of security and to know what it's like to be happy again. My maternal instinct said to give them time, so that's what I did.

On the outside, we were resuming a so-called normal life. But inside, we each felt the insurmountable loss, sadness, and confusion we carried with us. I remember walking our eldest son to the bus each morning, noticing how tightly he held my hand. As we waited, he would move his arms around my stomach and hold on tight. Always touching, poking, or hugging, I could see his need to connect. He was checking in to make sure I wasn't going anywhere. It was a safe way to defend against the void left by his father's absence. Hold on for dear life. Hold on to mama.

I remember the feeling of anxiety that would wash over me as I walked back to a quiet household. Seldom was I alone, but when I was, the quietness felt intolerable. Sometimes I felt like I was going to jump out of my own skin. Nighttime was the worst. Insomnia set in beginning the night he died. Underneath, the world suddenly felt unsafe. Terrible things did happen that were out of your control, and there were things that went bump in the night. I was also reminded that as a parent, I could not really protect my children from unforeseen dangers.

The fact that my ex-husband killed himself began to haunt me. I felt sickened at the level of despair he must have felt to the point of wanting to kill himself. Somewhere along the way, he stopped seeing the value of his life, the importance of his being. Somewhere along the way, he stopped feeling, remembering, and knowing how much he meant to others. How much he mattered to us. That broke my heart. Miserableness and heartbreak were taking their places at the table now. I suffered from the thought that he hurt himself and those around him. And I was struggling with all the choices he made leading up to that moment of suicide. So many bad choices. I was in a very uncomfortable place in my mind.

If I were to speak my truth honestly, I will never understand why he didn't come to me. Of all people he knew, of all the people who could help, it should have been me. In her book *Night Falls Fast, Understanding Suicide*, Kay Redfield Jamison wrote, "Because of privacy of my nightmare had been of my own designing, no one close to me had any real idea of the psychological company I had been keeping."

That is what this was, a deeply private companion no one knew about. How could I not have known about this? And how could he have not shared it with me with so much at stake? I was the counselor in his life, the one he had been closest to. And I was the one who could have rescued in the best way possible. Perhaps it was pride, or maybe anger. Clearly, he did not want rescuing. Perhaps having to ask for help was too much. Perhaps he couldn't stop the addiction. Maybe he came to believe we'd be better off without him. I was heartbroken he felt his life had no value or purpose. Even during the heated conflict of a divorce, I would have moved heaven and earth to help him with the addiction and keep him alive. I understood better than anyone the seriousness of an out-of-control addiction, the disturbing and painful addictive nature of methamphetamines, the difficulty of detox, the support that is needed, the difficulties in the recovery process, and the potential all along the way for self-destruction. Little did I know that suicide should have been part of the conversation and process.

Suicide is a conversation that needs to be had with another human being. Out of all conversations to have, this is the one to have with another. This is exactly what the Greek philosophers wrote about—the need to challenge someone's beliefs, hear another's perspective, think about something like life and death differently. There are so many layers to unpack when contemplating one's life. And in those moments, how critical it is to make a connection and have support around you. This is also one of the paradoxes of suicide. At the most critical time, when a person needs to connect with another the most, he or she simply doesn't.

In Alcoholics Anonymous they say, "You are as sick as your secrets." Tom's secrets were what led him to that final decision. What I know more than anything, which has always been the main driving force in me, was that our children needed him. He was irreplaceable. Even wounded, even scarred, even broken they would have loved him. At times I have so much compassion for him. I am sorry for his struggle. I am sorry for myself and for our children. I am sad for our friends and family, for the extended community around us who knew him. At times it has just felt like an insurmountable amount of loss. And as I have discovered this new journey of grief, I have felt something deeper inside, like I'm just starting to touch the edge of something that will not so easily go away.

Today I am rereading Kay Redfield Jamison's book about suicide. I've marked up the pages, quoted her here, and still I reread it. I'm still trying to make sense of things, learn something new. Develop a new level of understanding. The experts define my behavior as someone who is trying to find meaning. I would say find meaning and create some sort of understanding along the way. I have a dozen books on loss sitting at my feet. Stories, theories, and support. Some offer expertness in how to grieve. Thanks, but I've become an expert on that all on my own without even trying. To coin Stephen Jenkinson's term, "broken heartedness" runs in my veins now. According to Jungian typology, I am a feeling type. I have a thinking mind, too, but my feelings run strong, so loving and losing love impact my heart. And my heart often leads when it comes to love, so broken heartedness makes sense.

This is where I have lived these past few years since his death, in the valley of loss and broken heartedness. With Kay's book, reading and rereading. Reading and rereading. Contemplating, trying to understand. Make sense. Make sense. Make sense. And on some level, it never does.

I'd quote her whole book if I could. Instead, I search for those phrases that resonate in my soul. "The suffering of the suicidal is private and inexpressible."

Yes. I was five blocks away. The shock is inexpressible. I was five blocks away, and you killed yourself after you called me at 1:30 in the morning. I was your last phone call. You died a gruesome death. Unpalpable. Unpalatable. Inexpressible. There is the shock in the not knowing. Keeping such a deep dark secret from me, the woman you were married to all those years, the woman who is the mother of your children, the woman you spoke to hours before you died, telling her you'd see them—our children—tomorrow. The woman you called as you were killing yourself. Yes, me. I'm here. I saw the call registered on my phone. The one left behind to pick up all the pieces. Make sense of things. There, I found my anger again. Unbelievable. How could I ever possibly explain this to our children? How could you leave me with that burden? And how could you hand them this heavy stone of sadness to carry around for the rest of their lives? I thought you loved them. How are we supposed to move forward? How can I feel confident in taking charge when creatures like this come out in the darkness of night? When secrets like this are buried in your soul? And tell me, how can I keep our children safe?

They, the experts, say you have to get in touch with your anger when someone suicides. I have much to be angry at—why you did it, why you didn't come to me, why you would do this to our children. Judgment and anger dance together. Yes, you should have handled that better. You should have done better. Both of you. The judgment also launches itself at me. I should have done better. I could have done something, anything to prevent this. There is no resolution in this anger. Restless never-ending dialogue, forever pointing fingers.

There, the anger has been expressed. I got in touch with it. Now what? I know there is a complexity of feelings that arise from a tragedy like this. The therapist in me says it's OK to feel all of it. We have depth to us and our experiences. They are only feelings. Just keep an eye on the ones that stay and make you feel bitter. They can do damage to your stomach, to your sleep, to your mind, to your life story. Don't be bitter. Don't stay angry. Be sad, be heartbroken, be confused for a little while, and then surrender all of it. Surrender it to the vast universe around us, to the new pages of life being written as you read this, to the memories that will be permanently stored in your mind, to the newly formed legacy that has breached your border walls and now resides on your continent. This is all a new discovery. All of this land is yours, even the canyons that hold so much grief and unimaginable loss. It's all temporary anyway.

Where you used to be, there is a hole in the world, which I find myself constantly walking around in the daytime and falling in at night. I miss you like hell.

—Edna St. Vincent Millay

CHAPTER 8

HOW DO YOU GET OVER A LOVED ONE'S SUICIDE?

Around the world, the World Health Organization (WHO) reports that approximately 800,000 people die by suicide each year. It is a statistic we never hear about. What's worse, the impact of the suicide affects far more people beyond immediate family members. It impacts communities.

It can be incredibly difficult to find hope after a tragedy such as losing a loved one to suicide. Grief that is more difficult to process is what they call "complex grief," or, "complicated grief." There are many layers to it, and it affects a person's recovery and healing. It includes a change in someone's perspective and can include questions, shame, guilt, blame, anger, sadness, and confusion. The struggle toward healing can be seen in health issues a loved one experiences after the loss, in their search to find meaning and in the need to repurpose his or her views about what it means to be alive.

The most visceral thing I remember about the suicide was the shock. The shock created from the act of someone killing himself or herself is truly an unforgettable experience. It includes the realization that someone you know was suffering so much he or she needed to end it all. That fact alone can take a long time to come to terms with. And for some, it is never fully resolved. Suicide is a dramatic act, a very strong statement without words. For months, my first thought when I woke up was, *Tom is gone.* Then I would catch my breath as I added, *he committed suicide.* There would be a pause as I thought, *What just happened?* And then it would hit me. *Oh, my God, the children.* This wave of sadness would engulf me as I got out of bed to start the day. As Judith Herman describes, those in a suicidal state are, "rendered helpless by an overwhelming force." I would say that those surviving a loved one's suicide are also rendered helpless in a similar manner by an overwhelming sense of shock and subsequent trauma.

For the first three months following Tom's death, I wondered how I would survive his death because it felt so overwhelming. I honestly didn't think I'd be able to survive it, not because I wanted to die, but because the loss was so devastating. I simply could not imagine living a life without Tom. I couldn't picture it. There is something so visceral that happens when you are emotionally and physically connected to another human being.

A month after his death, I went to see a client on a hospital floor that had pneumonia patients. I was so out of my head with grief, I didn't even think about how contagious something like that could be. Shortly after that visit, I came down with pneumonia. I tried to power through with antibiotics, dismissing the illness. I had to work, and the children needed my attention. But that approach didn't work. Then one night, I had a dream about death. In it I was walking through a desert. The wind was howling, stirring up so much sand that it was hard to see. Everything was black and white. I strained to push against the wind in a futile attempt to move forward, and I could feel that I was losing the fight. I realized everything around me was dead, and I was not in a place I wanted to be. Terrified, I woke up and consciously choose to live. I had been so immersed in grief; I saw I had to change my mindset and think about living. I had to consciously live in the moment. For the sake of my children and for my life that I have loved, I created a mantra I recited daily. Then I started a second round of antibiotics and promised myself I would fight and survive. And I have.

Memories were the second things that stood out to me in this grief process. Suicide can be traumatizing. I found myself replaying situations and conversations, reviewing dates, mulling over things with wonderings. These were memories but also symptoms of post-traumatic stress disorder. I was reliving my experiences of that fateful day, along with the events that led up to that day and the days following. It was like there was a video on replay in my head. This was my mind's attempt to make sense of what happened and to find a way to integrate something so unusual into my narrative of living. Something unexpected, unexplained, unfathomable had just happened. How was I going to make sense of that? Some of those memories and that process turned out to be pages of this book.

The third thing that I remember was the grief. A quote I had read on the AllianceofHope.com website said, "You never get over the loss from suicide, you have to learn to live with it." Initially, that had sounded like an excuse someone had made up. I had been trained in a linear counseling paradigm, the traditional pathology model in clinical psychology. Things were either one way or the other. If you had a problem, it was either worked through and you moved past it, or you got stuck and it disabled you. You needed to get over the grief. And how wrong I was. How wrong that paradigm is. I have since learned that grief is not a pathology, and a loss like this is not something you just get over; you have to learn to live with it. And sometimes it takes longer than expected.

I stuck to my training. I told myself that whoever wrote that just needed a great therapist, some good cognitive restructuring, and a strong spiritual practice, and they would be fine. They would move on and follow the parameters our culture dictated as the right way to grieve and the right way to live. The *get over it model* included the shortest route of grieving with as little suffering as possible for the grieving person and for those around them. Not necessarily the best or healthiest way to go. At the time, I was not aware that my rigid thinking was a way of defending against the immensity of this loss. Reconciling and forgiveness were needed because a loved one had suicided.

In response to reading that quote, I immediately set out to prove that statement untrue. I would get over it and show everyone, whoever everyone was. I stayed in my own therapy, found my children counselors, wrote in my journal, attended church, prayed, practiced meditation, exercised, volunteered in the community, connected with friends, and performed well at work. Being busy helped keep grief at bay. But a year went by, and the grief was still there. I was as determined as ever to move on, so another year passed with this busy agenda of living I had developed. And still, there was an ever-present feeling of loss with his absence. What was also surfacing was not just the loss but the existential implications of what it means when someone suicides. All the questions that come up after someone suicides. Topics related to a suicide presented themselves, like why we are here, why we stay alive, why we make certain choices in our lives, and what our value systems are. All the shadows of suicide, all the details, and all the stigmas also took up regular space in my mind and in my living. They always seemed to be there.

While writing for SAVE.org, an organization for suicide survivors, Robin Chodrak received the message that she should write about her loss and her process of grief. In her book *Be Gentle with Me, I'm Grieving*, Robin wrote, "Based on my experiences, with grief I can say that death by suicide is like none other." I thought she wrote that for me because I had just landed there. I began to understand that three years after his death, when I really started to feel the depth of the loss and the profoundness of the act of suicide itself. I was struggling at that point, trying to understand why I was still grieving. I had done all the right things. It should have been fixed. But it wasn't.

In Dr. Robert Shabahangi's book *Ambiguity of Suffering*, he writes of "the ambiguity of pathos (suffering)" to emphasize that suffering is a valid, real way to experience life. And it is not something to just pathologize away or stay busy to avoid. Suffering is an experience in and of itself, a human experience that we must delve into. When we acknowledge the suffering and stay with it, "The experience adds a depth to our understanding of our place in the world and deepens the relationship we have with ourselves." In other words, my grief was about to become a landmark piece of work for me. I just had to learn how to be with it.

A friend remembered being told that she needed to "get over" her brother's suicide. That response dumbfounded her. The norm of our culture dictated she needed to move past the thing that brought sadness and discomfort. The thing most profound. As anyone who has lost a loved one knows, the last thing she wanted to do was stop thinking about her beloved brother. Thinking was the only thing she had left of him to hold on to. She was so bereft with grief, she remembered she couldn't smile because she thought being happy would somehow mean she was forgetting him.

As Gary Roe says, "You must get good at grief." My experience of grief has since moved me from the pathological model of living and diagnosing my grief process to a consciousness model, one where all experiences we feel are valid and important parts of our experiences. I feel like I've gotten good at grief. This includes the conscious act of being with your real process, whatever it is. These moments become necessary landmarks for personal growth and development. The things that happen—or the way we experience them—don't always make sense, but all serve a purpose. If only, as Dr. Shabahangi expresses, to deepen our experiences of ourselves.

One day I found the original quote from the Alliance of Hope website and realized Tom's suicide was not something for me to get over but something I would have to learn to *live with*. I had thought that getting over it also meant getting over him, and that meant to say goodbye to him permanently, which I found I was not ready to do. I realized that I needed more time with him, with my memories of him, with missing him, with the grief in our family. As I came to this realization, a huge sense of relief fell over me as I became aware that I was never going to get over it, but I didn't have to. I also didn't have to say goodbye to him in such a permanent and forgettable way. Tom's suicide would always be with me, just as Tom would always be with me. I just had to develop a new relationship with my process of grieving, with losing him, and with trying to understand what his suicide meant to me.

I also had to learn how to be with him in memory only. That was one of the hardest things. And it still is. That included learning to live with a void that held the absence of his being. Live with the suffering. Live with the empty place he had filled in our lives. Live with all the empty spaces that were to come. There were so many ways our lives were intertwined. So many layers to sift through. He was still very much with us, and I needed to be with that.

My focus then shifted as I deepened my understanding of loss. I began to start doing something different, almost counterculture: I started to embrace the grief and the sense of loss. I welcomed it and started to look at how I could be with his suicide and his absence. Not in the sense of letting it take over my life, but more of just being OK with whatever space I was in when I thought of him, his death, or the topic of suicide. I learned to accept my grief as something that existed in my life as much as living and breathing do. I also became OK with the ambiguity of loss. How amorphous, unpredictable, and deep it is. At that point, my grieving became much easier. It was a huge relief to let go of trying to grieve the "right" way. This shift has also allowed me to be more present with my children's grief. I now know there is no timeline or right way to do it. It just is. Whenever and wherever. My job is to show up in the moment and be with it.

Wrangling the Disappointment of Suicide

Suicide impacts people in ways you can't possibly imagine.

It leaves unanswered questions that open the door for disappointment to set up shop as a permanent resident—why the person didn't come to you for help, why they did it, why they left, how could they have been that unhappy without you knowing. How someone you thought you knew, someone you thought was like you, with the same worldview, same belief in God, same way of walking through the world would suddenly end their life. Someone you thought you could count on. Someone you thought would be around for a while. Someone who helped shape your experience of the world, someone who was an integral part of your world, suddenly absent.

No warning, no goodbye, just gone.

Certain types of shock and life endings leave lingering emotions. I often see disappointment in my children's eyes when we talk about their father. It's an ongoing wondering how they could be living so much life without him. How is it that their father, not their friends' fathers, but their father did this? How could he have knowingly picked this outcome? Didn't he love them, want to be with them? They experience missing, loss, disappointment.

Elisabeth Kübler-Ross called the final stage of grief acceptance or reconciliation. I would argue that with some forms of tragic loss, family members never get to a place of reconciliation. It's more a resignation with a permanent layer of disappointment. Even with the best rational or psychological explanation, something so terrible doesn't get so easily reconciled. When dealing with loss on this deep level, it doesn't matter if it was drugs, mental illness, and so on. The cause is irrelevant. It's just stuck there in your mind as an image or thought: *my loved one committed suicide.*

In some ways, it is permanently unexplainable. So much loss can be too much to bear, too much to make sense of. And it gets catalogued in our psyches in different ways. I've heard stories about families who change after losing a loved one to suicide. Sometimes a person starts approaching life with an air of indifference or becomes apathetic. Or some people develop an inability to attach or stay in meaningful relationships. Perhaps they become permanently depressed. Others may appear perpetually angry and display outward bursts of unsettledness. Some family members become anxious with a fearful outlook on life. Sometimes the family system takes a downward spiral, and the family breaks up. Or alcoholism sets up residence. One family was described as falling apart as every family member developed an addiction and subsequent mental illness. Not outcomes I think anyone would expect or ask for.

With suicide, there is no explanation that makes it OK because it's a suicide. The fact of the matter is that the suicide of loved one is almost always not OK. It's blatantly obvious that is the point of the suicide. It can often be an act of anger, an act to make a statement. It can be an action that is intended to harm, to get people to think, to think about that person, what they did, who they were, and how they'll be missed. When suicide is done out of anger, revenge, or pure suffering, it's a form of lashing out. And it works, even though it's a terrible solution.

A pain that started in Tom's childhood was brought back up with the divorce and loss of my parents, exacerbated by an addiction, and then acted out with his death. Suicide reverberates pain, sending waves of it out into the universe. It was reverberated in our house, with our family, and with the extended community around us. His death extended emotionally and geographically, and it impacted people on different continents.

Suicide can leave a legacy of sadness. What I can say from parenting our children these last few years is that Tom's suicide brought a layer of sadness, anger, confusion, and disappointment that can't be taken away. The divorce is something we could have all survived. His death would have taken a while, but we would have been OK. But death by suicide brought a whole other layer, a deeper layer of suffering. If I am to speak my truth here, there was a shattering of innocence when our children found out that their father committed suicide. It created this experience in them that has been really terrible. This traumatic event permanently changed their views of themselves, their father, and their perceptions of the world around them. And that is one of the few things I have been unable to forgive Tom for.

I know that on some level, they will never get over the fact that their father committed suicide. And that's painful to say. I can only hope they will somehow, perhaps through their own spiritual paths, each find a way to make sense of it and reconcile it in their own ways that will allow them to go on living and be at peace. It's just disappointing and so unsettling.

One of the dirty secrets about suicide is that it basically tells everyone the person was not OK. The day the boys found out their father committed suicide, they also found out he didn't just die; he killed himself because he was not OK. That's scary stuff for children to find out. Not only was he not OK, but he was also struggling and desperate. And there was nothing they could do about it. Thanks to their father, they also learned and experienced what an extreme act of desperation looks like.

This is a complicated legacy to leave. It often forces loved ones to sift through all sorts of topics, like the grisly details of how the loved one died, where responsibility lies, all the consequences or fallout that happened, and the long-term outcomes no one could have possibly foreseen. It sets a series of events in motion that can be very difficult for those left behind. And the review can be very painful. The suicide in our family was sudden and unexpected. What I know is that for the last few years of his life, I was in a relationship with a man who had a sick state of mind due to a growing and serious drug addiction. I witnessed the start of it, the initial signs. And then watched as it developed and took over his life. Suicide was never something that concerned me. It never even occurred to me because he was always fighting to see his children.

What I also know is that when the drugs took over, and insanity became a way of being, there was no way for me or the kids to maneuver in that space. There was little room for us. It was like we were being squeezed out of our relationships with him, replaced with other things as part of a self-destructive pattern that became his new way of living. I knew things would have to get worse before they got better. But even then, suicide was never a viable option and was never mentioned. There were no blatant signs, no comments, no conversations, just a lot of stressors adding up. And still, I held hope because that man loved his children. He kept fighting to see them. That was one of the few constants in his life. This tells me that on some level, he was trying to stay alive. That is why he was struggling so; part of him was self-destructing, and part of him was trying to survive. What a conflict. Suicide didn't fit the picture or his profile, even in a drug-induced state. It was hidden, deeply hidden.

This is the other part of the dirty secrecy suicide carries with it. It exposes how twisted our minds can get. When we become too self-centered, we become both the victim and the perpetrator. It becomes all about us, and we become everything. Everyone else gets squeezed out. Others' thoughts, feelings, and needs no longer exist. The mind becomes distorted, and the perspective becomes one sided. Singular. In the process, we lose our connections with others, which can sometimes be lifelines, voices of reason, or reminders of a reason to keep living. Or a reason to talk to someone. Ask for advice or help. To hold hope. Challenge our deeply held beliefs and our rational thoughts. To rethink things.

As clear as he was about the self-destructive direction he was heading in, Tom became very disconnected from the people he loved the most—his family, friends, and his children. Our children sure didn't need this. He could have never predicted how the children would survive losing him. I am assuming on some level he had fantasies about dying and what his death would mean to everyone. What they would say about him, what they would think. But he couldn't possibly have known what the real outcome would be for any of us. Another bitter pill for me to swallow. What I do know, without a doubt, is that he never would have considered suicide (with a sober mind) if he had known the long-lasting, perhaps permanent, pain and suffering he would cause in his children. That is a painful realization.

If I could guess any regrets he has right now, wherever he is, he would not have wanted that for anyone he loved, especially our boys. This book is about him, but it's also about those of us still here. And it's about how our family is moving on from his suicide. I can testify that the boys' suffering continues. And it is something they will have to continue to reconcile. In the same breath, I can say we are also doing that, each in our way. Life continues to move on without him because we are the survivors. With time comes a silver lining of potentiality. It's in love, in relationships, in time passing, and one's natural ability to heal. It's in the heart space we hold, in the new forms of hope we develop, and in those sudden bursts of laughter.

I can say that we are also healing each other. There is a duality there. They suffer, we suffer, and at the same time, I know now that we are all going to be OK. We will survive this.

My internal struggle continues as I feel a divide in me, at times feeling compassion for the suffering my ex-husband was going through and for the loss he experienced by acting so radically and recklessly. I struggle with forgiveness as I feel the level of suffering that must have been going on in him for this to have happened. Then I feel my anger as I see our children hurting. Hurting unnecessarily. Struggling, struggling unnecessarily. I see my work is to help with the healing and reconciliation, starting with my own forgiveness. To teach them how to temper my and their disappointments. Help make sense of things. Show them factors of living—the beauty in being alive, the power of choice, of taking responsibility, of loving, of caring, of being in relationships with others. And the importance of asking for help, of choosing peace, hope, and happiness. As I struggle, I carry their pain when I can. I pray for hope, compassion, forgiveness, and for some way to reconcile all this because regardless of the reason, suicide is an incredibly selfish act.

Suicide with All Its Questions

One of the many by-products of suicide are all the questions, questions about things you normally would not think of. Tom's suicide recently left me wondering about his soul. It's a new level of worry and concern I never had for him before. Of the family and friends, I have known and lost, all have passed peacefully, except for Tom. His was a tragic, chosen, and violent ending. What happens now?

In Buddhist theory, the state of mind the person is in at the time of death is important and impacts the quality of his or her life at rebirth. They suggest to live well and die well, live happy and die happy to have a positive rebirth experience. If it is in a karmic cycle our souls live, then perhaps suicide is a pit stop, a hiccup forcing the soul to go back and do it again, but this time, the right way. They also believe in cycles of karmic suicide. If a person suicides, they will have to work on that for several lifetimes.

Some belief systems describe those who have suicided are sent into a state of limbo and reside in this permanent state between worlds. It's described as dark, lonely, isolating, a different dimension. Some who survived their suicide attempts claim to have seen or experienced this place. They describe it as being stuck in corners, alone, sitting there in a dark room, and in a perpetual state of penance, regret, and sadness. Countless others who have died and been resuscitated or have had near-death experiences describe seeing a light, seeing loved ones, and being given a message. Some who have survived suicide attempts have described where they went as an awakening with a benevolent God there to greet them and offer the love, forgiveness, and support they needed.

I don't know what or who to believe. To be honest, I never really needed an answer until I had someone in my life die a violent death. Suicide is often committed by someone in an altered state of mind, leaving an unsettled soul passing into another realm. Now I frequently wonder what that means.

In a traditional Christian sense, some believe everything that happens to us happens to prepare us to be with our Creator. Bearing witness and sitting with those who suffer is one lesson. Maybe some need to learn more about compassion. The actual suffering is the lesson for others. Regardless of the lessons we each must learn in this life, many people think that something happens after we die. Our souls go somewhere. Where or what we do next, we just don't know.

I've been calling on my spiritual faith these past few years to tell me things are OK with Tom. I want the universe to send me a sign that despite those years of addiction, bad choices, and struggles, he is OK now. I look at images in a tarot card reading or a message that comes to me in a dream. I look through the Bible for that one quote that will pull it all together for me. I want an answer from the universe tied up tight with a bow, easy to figure out and clear as day. I want an assurance that everything is OK, that he is OK. Instead, I get no assurances from the world around me or from another realm. No dream, no intuition, no quote, no answer. I've developed a new type of worry; I wonder where his soul is after such an angry, violent death. I wonder if he is OK or still struggling. I wonder if he is angry or alone. I wonder if his spirit is perpetually stuck in somewhere, never to be seen again. I often wonder where he is and what process he must go through now to heal. Or if he even gets that as an option.

Our culture talks openly about aggression in relation to others. I wonder if we get punished for aggression toward ourselves. We hear about victims in the news, how some perpetrator injured or killed a victim. We learn about military exercises in history books that are filled with violence. It's justified killing. Soldiers killing soldiers, or civilians for a reason. Killing with a rationale, a purpose. We learn that there is a right way to die and a wrong way to die. Just like there is a right way to kill or be killed. Random acts of violence are not OK. Suicide is not OK. Seldom do we acknowledge violent aggression against the self. Suicide is the darkest and most aggressive form of violence against oneself. The intent is to do serious damage; it's to annihilate oneself. But it's somehow seen as less terrible because it's inflicted on the self instead of on another. If we value the experience of living and value and care about all sentient beings, those inflicting are still in as much in danger as those receiving violence. Both seem terrible to me.

I wonder where Tom's soul went and what he is doing now. Does he get to be with this his loved ones? Does he get to meet the saints or God and angels he once loved and believed in? Does he get to pass through the pearly white gates as Catholicism describes? Is St. Peter there to greet him? Or is it another place? Perhaps it's like Hades, with Thanatos standing there waiting for him. Maybe it's another place he goes to, one for the less fortunate, those with troubles, those who chose to commit the sin of all sins against their God—the taking of a life. That's what we were taught; suicide was a sin against God. Life is a gift from God and is not ours to take. It's one thing to learn these concepts in a theoretical way but another to live it. Tom suicided. What happens now? Do they go to the reality they chose to believe in during that final moment of death? Do we really create our own afterlife? Did he go into that gray area between heaven and hell? Did he start a direct descent into the seven levels? Is there someone there to meet him? Do they get a talking to instead and maybe offered a penance or some type of healing? Is there a priest or angel there to confess to, or are they truly alone? I wonder, *Does the person who suicided understand what has happened, and what price one has to pay? And why do I feel so responsible for his death? Why do I carry this burden?* I find this is common with those who loved someone who suicided. We often carry some type of survivor guilt. We should have done more. We should have been there to help prevent all of this.

My guilt and unsettledness sit on my shoulders padded with regrets. My ego thinks I should have prevented it, that I had the power over his choice to live or die. It's arrogant to think that, and not rational. It's not logical and doesn't make sense, but I think it anyway. I think it's easier to blame yourself or someone else than to sit with the powerlessness we feel when someone we love kills himself or herself. It's such a statement and such a final act; it's so powerful. How could I have prevented this?

Since Tom's passing, I seldom have a normal night's sleep. My soul remains in a state of unrest on some deep level. Try as I might to create a healthy lifestyle, eat right, exercise, work on hobbies, manage stress, and have a strong and healthy mindset, I never sleep normally. And I am always awake now at 1:30 a.m. It's a restlessness that set in the moment he died. It has settled way down, but it is still there. And it's often at 1:30 a.m. or when I am automatically woken up that it returns, and I start thinking about Tom again. In my favorite rescue fantasy, the one with the best outcome, he calls and I pick up the phone and answer.

That night I did hear the phone ring. And I chose not to answer it. Then when I decided to pick it up, he had already hung up. Tom didn't leave a message. I've always wondered what it would have been like had I spoken to him. I can't imagine what he would have said: "I'm just calling to tell you that I'm killing myself"? Maybe he would have raged at me again, blaming me for everything. Perhaps he would have said, "I'm sorry." One never knows when methamphetamines, depression, and rage are at play.

I know that if I had answered the phone and figured out that he was in trouble, I would have taken action. He knew that. And he knew that any outcome would have been difficult. Even for an addict, suicidal, and in a psychotic state, getting help can breed more anger and resentment. It was much easier and more effective to keep the drug addiction alive and blame others rather than take responsibility for the addiction and problems he caused. Even if he had gotten help, I know he would have resented me more, probably hated me, and kept using. Maybe he would not have answered the door if I had gone over there. I just know I wanted Tom to live. I just wanted a chance for him to stay alive. To live for one more day, one more week. Have a chance to stay alive, get clean and sober, clear his head, and see that he had options and friends and a family who still cared about him.

I wanted a chance for hope.

To the world you may be one person, but to one person you are the world.

—Hellofund.org

CHAPTER 9

ANOTHER MILESTONE AFTER DEATH

Katy Perry plays through our house these days. I can tell the boys miss their father; they carry an invisible blanket of depression around them. Like Mary Pipher said, "I steer people away from the idea happiness is connected to having more, more, and more." I, too, normally steer away from that, but lately, I have been instinctively buying them things in an effort to throw off the blanket. Their hearts have been broken. Money and objects can't heal this loss. It doesn't work, but I try anyway. Sometimes instinct trumps rational.

Looking on the surface, our lives have resumed a normal routine. Our youngest son has grown a foot and gone up two shoe sizes in the past six months. He carries his father's build. Our eldest is now styling his hair the same way his father did. I buy him the same hair gel I bought my husband for so many years. He tells me about Emma Stone winning a Nickelodeon Kid's Choice Award. I ask him how he knows who Emma Stone is.

"Oh, Mom, she is Spider-Man's girlfriend."

Spider-Man doesn't have a name, but his girlfriend does. It's Emma Stone.

"She's pretty," he says.

Puberty is starting.

They tell me about all sorts of things. Unlike many of their friends who don't talk to their parents, my kids tell me almost everything. We talk about their friendships, the things they find funny, games they play, the latest cell phones they want, money, buying another house, future jobs, laws, police, the difference between right and wrong, elephants becoming extinct, how babies are made, Minecraft, hacking, and TV shows. My oldest asks when he will get chest hair, how cavities develop, and who is playing in the World Cup.

We talk about what to say to their friends when it comes to their father's death. Friends are a big deal. Margo Requarth notes in *After a Parent's Suicide, Helping children to Heal,* children need to be able to talk about the tragedy and be able to tell their friends, so they do not carry the burden of the tragedy alone. I have supported them in their own therapy as one place to talk about it, and I have supported them with how they tell this story to their friends. I don't want them to feel more alienated or different than they already are. But as Rachel Simmons observes in *Odd Girl Out: The Hidden Culture of Aggression in Girls,* one task for teens/tweens is learning how to put words to such an emotionally charged experience. They need to be able to express such an important loss. Fortunately, their friends were also our closest family friends and already knew what happened, making the conversations short and resolved. And as is so typical with boys, the question was asked, answered, and done with in under thirty seconds.

Margo Requarth wrote, "People are often uncomfortable talking about someone who died by suicide. They are concerned that such conversations will evoke too much emotion. But a child needs to hear those who loved her parent talk openly without idealizing or blaming the departed." Even at this stage, I still have questions thrown at me constantly. Questions such as, is their father in heaven with God? When will they get to see him again? Where is he exactly? How come they can't see him? My heart pangs as I see them struggle to make sense of this tragedy. Then the conversation turns again to something lighter.

"Are Goldfish crackers considered junk food?"

"If we had a million dollars like Batman, would we be able to have a butler too?"

"When will I be able to drive?"

"Do you think I'll be a good dad some day?"

The conversation eventually shifts back to dying. What would happen to them if I died? Where would they go to live? I reassure, I educate, I try. There is so much to teach them and so much to listen to. Each day I pick them up and get a fifteen-minute download about how their days went, good or bad. It includes who they met and what they talked about. They admit their mistakes, and we move forward together towards evening. We are all tired at the end of the day. My patience is short, so I learn to pick my battles. I'm a single parent now, on duty 24/7, and I have to try to stay as even keel as possible. Since their father's passing, I've been reading a lot about addiction and suicide with the hope that being informed will give me confidence. Even with my degrees, training, and years of therapy, suicide is a hard thing to make sense of. And it's harder to heal.

What I have learned is that they lost a primary male attachment figure, and that's a huge loss. John Bolby, the founder of attachment theory, said the two deepest emotional experiences humans feel are attachment and loss. My children just experienced both. They will develop other relationships, but their father will never be replaced. So much is absorbed in relationships and in the day-to-day living. They will miss so many opportunities. I also see they are aware they are missing a father figure. I fight like a vigilante to prevent more loss, loss of identity or loss of self-esteem. I tell them how important they are. I teach them that where we live is our home, and the three of us are a family unit now. I teach them to be careful who they talk to. I urge them to watch the choices they make. They will have to grow up faster now because as a single working parent, I won't always be able to be there for them. I tell them they are loved, they matter, and they are here on this earth for a reason. I was under the false impression that after the first year, with therapy, church, a stable routine, talking about their father's death, setting up rituals, and having time to heal would help the grief subside, but it hasn't. I have two young boys who have lost their father. A big part of their world has simply been destroyed.

Some of the greatest battles will be fought within the silent chambers of your own soul.

—Ezra Taft Benson

CHAPTER 10

THE MARRIAGE OF ADDICTION AND SUICIDE

Because someone survives the loss of a loved one doesn't mean he or she doesn't get broken or wounded in the process. They can become damaged, confused, unsure about things. They can lose their way or their identity. They can miss key developmental milestones. Devastating loss can put someone in an existential spiral and make the individual wonder why he or she is here. This is especially true for children. If no one is there to explain it and help a child to understand, children will put the pieces together themselves in whatever discombobulated, inaccurate manner that works. They will build their own scripts and narratives, which become the stories they then tell themselves and others. These stories become their truths simply because they were the narratives, they were able to craft. Brené Brown shared her thoughts: "Sometimes the most dangerous thing for kids is the silence that allows them to construct their own stories—stories that almost always cast them as alone and unworthy of love and belonging."

When families divorce, parents are often counseled to tell their children that they are not the cause of the divorce. Children, naturally egocentric, assume it's their fault or that they could have prevented it. For children who lose a parent or both parents at a young age, not only can death become an interruption in their development, it also impacts their ideas about how the world works. What was once a safe world might not feel so safe. The space in their beings, where their needs were once met, might now be filled with loneliness and feelings of abandonment. Some have fight-or-flight responses, while some withdraw. Ana Freud described the responses of children in orphanages after Germany invaded Europe as rocking themselves, refusing to eat, banging their heads against the wall, and unable to speak.

Others had a loss of mobility, while some had no sense of purpose. A variation of what I would call a failure to thrive, or perhaps a failure to survive.

If we look at Tom's suicide from a more psychological perspective, this is really where Tom's story began. I suspect now that from a few rare comments he made to me over the years, his suicidality started when his parents died. He had eleven years of living in a loving household with a strong, solid family. Suddenly, with no warning, he was abruptly torn away from his mother, who died from cancer. Then a few years later, cancer hit again, resulting in the death of his father. His world went from love and security to loss, abandonment, and aloneness. It was like he became one of those children in that orphanage. How could he possibly comprehend or come to reckon the loss of both parents? With no warning, no explanation, no sense of safety, how could he make sense of having his family torn apart? What kind of God would do that? How would he see the world after that? And how could he survive it?

This is really not my story to tell. It's Tom's story. But it is such an integral part of our story and our marriage that it warrants some mention. Tom died as someone who lost his father at an early age. Our eldest son was almost the same age as Tom was when he unexpectedly said goodbye to his father. That's how close these narratives run together. In some ways, they are not related, but in other ways, they are inextricably connected. Tom lost both of his parents. And it was devastating. Our children have lost their father, and it's been devastating for them. That much I know.

We could speculate that losing both parents was so terrifying and overwhelming that it opened the possibility for him to seek drugs to self-soothe. After Tom's death, I learned that during his teen years, his depression was aided by cocaine and methamphetamine addictions. Depression from the losses, anxiety from being alone in a big world, and an addiction to mask the pain and confusion. With that came a period of suicide ideation.

I am guessing that when Tom's parents died, some part of him wished that he had died too. I think that is when the suicide script started and where the wound was opened for an addiction to take hold. My point is not about what happened or didn't happen. It's that when someone gets to the point of suicide, not always, but often, there is some history, something in his or her life, events, thoughts, beliefs, and history that no one gets to hear. It is a story that has led them up to that moment. And as a culture, it's our duty to hear these stories and bear witness. And try to understand.

Perhaps Tom developed a script about wanting to die to be with his parents, and that is what became a deeply buried and deeply held belief system. Something he told himself for years; something that he believed to his core. It is not uncommon for children to want to die when their parent(s) have died. As adults, our cognitive abilities eventually allow us to differentiate between literal and metaphorical experiences, something a child's mind cannot always accomplish. Adults can usually intervene and put that perspective into symbolic context.

On some level, his life had no real value or meaning because his parents were gone. I suspect that was what was buried under the conflict in our marriage, his anxiety, the drug addiction, and later all the rage that surfaced. Toward the end of his life, in the heat of conflict and issues, it resulted in a suicide pact he made with himself. In some way, Tom had to prove to himself that he didn't deserve to live. He should die. The script said that the suffering and unhappiness were too difficult, those around him would be better off without him, and that he had no reason to live. He didn't really deserve to. What is so poignant to me is that if there was a script like this, it was not just about dying but also about his existence. He felt he had no real purpose for being here. In his mind, his life lacked meaning. Deep stuff and hard to get at.

As a teenager, he began using drugs to push away the sadness and anger. He depended on meth for a few years, found Narcotics Anonymous (NA), and stayed in the program for ten years. Solid sobriety, clarity of mind, NA meetings, and a few years of therapy. When he and I met, he had left all that, had done his work, and felt he could make it on his own. He was open and honest. He felt that he had the skills. He had learned how to live clean and sober, he had a sense of purpose, had worked on his grief, and could now live life on his terms. And he did for almost twenty years.

The high addictive energy I noticed during our marriage was never destructive or harmful. He had focus on things that were normed OK. He put it into making a successful marriage and career. He was passionate about things in an eccentric way. It wasn't just about coffee; it had to be a special brew from Pete's. It was that special recipe for Chicken Parmesan, or a Miles Davis CD that he loved. It was popular artwork or that new model Porsche. It was the collection of *Star Wars* movies, and those Harman Cardon speakers that made those movies sound amazing. He carried an excitement about living with this energy, and it was good energy to be around. Eventually, a lot of this energy was channeled into the technology that he sold for companies. And that passion paid off as he moved up the corporate ladder.

Tom had many hobbies and interests; some he was just more passionate about. Lines can get blurry when it comes to deciding what culturally condoned habits and interests are addictions. And according to our culture, there is nothing wrong being addicted to coffee or technology.

He had learned over the years that being a successful salesman was a good lifestyle for him. For one thing, it kept him busy. Because of a commute, Tom lived on coffee and listened to music after working long hours. Working in sales led to working weekends with overtime. The travel kept him unusually busy and achieving. Bringing in those dollars was the new drug, either bringing praise or disappointment. After we met, the cigarette smoking was replaced with a passion for cell phones and tech products. The videophile lifestyle was replaced with a home and a family and sales positions in the Silicon Valley. We incorporated more downtime into his off hours. We traveled and took off on short weekend trips. Sales paid the bills, which added an extra urgency to it. The sales industry is known for its incentive model, and naturally, they dangled more carrots at him. He liked those challenges.

With the bonus structures, he was able to buy even better things he was passionate about while still providing for his family. So the desire to achieve was always there. He liked achieving. He was good at it and did very well. Achieving made everyone happy. There were no bipolar symptoms; he wasn't manic or depressed. Tom was happy and emotionally balanced.

The leaps in his career kept happening after we married, and then the promotion came with a Fortune 50 company. The position was a stepping-stone to an international executive VP position they were grooming him for. He was now on the fast track. He had taken that position thinking he could keep the same routine and lifestyle he had maintained as a sales manager and just make more money. He was going to beat the system—work less but make more money. Unfortunately, it didn't work like that.

The changes I saw happened during the second year. He had traveled thirty-two weeks, and things were not looking as though they were going to let up. Work was more demanding than before. They added new continents; he was expected to grow them and keep the sales coming in. It was a huge amount of pressure for a new sales director. That first year he brought in 10 million dollars. The second year was a struggle. The travel was anywhere from four days to three weeks at a time, from the United States to Canada, Mexico, Asia, and South America. I always felt the company, as generous as it was, could have helped him with support in so many other ways. There was so much support needed in the day-to-day operations of running such a large division. He was bringing them in huge revenue. He was worth the support.

Instead, they withheld a bonus that year. The first big hit. That act started the decline I saw in his motivation for work. The money was not all there this time. The bonuses were what kept him going. They made it worth all the work. They were an extra incentive, a nice "Thank you." By my standards, it was a silly battle to have with an employee. Battling over a $20K bonus for a growing $10 million division seemed like a waste of resources and priorities. They took their eyes off the ball and their salesperson. Instead, they focused on dollars, on numbers. In doing that, they lost something they couldn't recoup, Tom's passion for the work. His passion was what drove the growth. Another hit. This time to his identity and self-esteem. By withholding the bonus, they, in not so many words, also told their rising star that his work and his talents weren't really worth it to them. Not a good message to send.

This is when I think he started using again. I remember a particular trip to Brazil because of the crazy flight times. The meetings started late at night and went through until early morning. He would call at odd hours when he could but couldn't wait to get home. He made the deals he needed to. I suspect drugs were offered somewhere along the way during that trip because something was different when he returned. He came home unusually exhausted. He was expected to be at work the following Monday, but he didn't make it. Instead, he took two sick days and slept straight through them. That was the first time in thirteen years I saw him take a sick day. There were no little bags of white powder, no beady eyes, no changes in mood, no stereotypic identifiers we have been taught to look for. All I saw was exhaustion. Yet, I could feel something was happening, I just wasn't sure what. Things always moved quickly with Tom, and it was sometimes hard to keep up.

I called his addiction "Mistress Meth" because it felt like a mistress in our marriage—silent, invisible, slowing and quietly influencing areas of his life. Often it felt like someone else was in the room with us, silently manipulating outcomes.

I think there was a combination of events that eventually unhinged him. The stress from work, combined with losing my parents and starting a meth addiction, were the foundations for the problems that arose. Losing the bonus, along with an increase in travel and difficulties on the home front with both of us grieving really strained our marriage. I was trying to focus on closing my parents' estate and managing a household with a toddler, baby, and absent father. Grieving made it difficult for both of us to attend to each other and address the events that were happening. We started fighting more and spending less time together. Death, grief, loss. Aloneness and unreconciled stuff about his parents' deaths probably surfaced again, overlaying day-to-day life. Now added was heavy stress from work, thus creating the perfect storm.

Depression followed. It came out as anger. As he got angrier, I retreated more. The depression was there. I noticed it as he became angrier more often and slept for longer periods of time. This was when Mistress Meth moved her way into our home, first into our money house. New behaviors started, ones that were not there to help the marriage or support a family. Then people from his past suddenly started showing up. People who used drugs and alcohol excessively. They connected with him while avoiding me.

Separation became a topic of conversation in moments of fighting. Mistress Meth was slowly weaving her way through our lives and destroying us. We tried counseling, unsure how to move forward. The sudden angry outbursts I could handle, but when the raging started, followed by bizarre behavior, I filed for a legal separation. Without identifying the growing addiction, counseling would never work. Nor would a marriage.

When we separated, Tom was hit with another big loss, the loss of a marriage. Losing a primary attachment during a time like this must have felt very ungrounding. We had been very close, and even amid the separating energies, our marriage was a foundation for both of us. He was losing his best friend and his family in the middle of all the stress in his life. His response was to nurture a growing addiction that would never give him the satisfaction he wanted or fulfill his needs.

Sometimes unresolved loss can become crippling when other events pile on top of it. The addiction also served a second purpose—managing all the energy required for his work. In the middle of all this, the pressure was still on to perform at work. He had to bring in the sales. That year, the travel increased. His performance was expected regardless of what was happening in his personal life. I suspect that the loss of our marriage was the catalyst that molded itself into a marriage of depression and addiction, where Mistress Meth stationed herself. This also helped keep the depression and anxiety at bay, while Mistress Meth settled in.

I'm sure for brief periods, the drugs made everything feel OK. Until they didn't. Only later would I learn that this way of coping was a repeated one from his teenage years—depression with the drugs that would eventually lead to suicidality. The trifecta of a deeply ingrained pattern, narrative, and mindset. Whatever the scripts and beliefs were, they stayed in his head and never became something he was willing to look at or share with me, his friends, or a trained professional.

The addiction he used to appease all of that was now causing more loss for him. The door had been reopened. With outbursts of rage and erratic behavior came restraining orders, a permanent loss of the marriage, custodial loss of his children, loss of our home, loss of his career, all our savings, and ultimately, disintegration of a life he had created and lived for so many years.

As he kept using and the addiction increased, the losses continued. These are the factors they say to watch for when someone is suicidal. These events can drive them to the edge. Tom was in a new place in his life, and it was not one in which he wanted to be. I suspect in what felt like an untenable state, suicide became the next option. What I do know is that never once did he acknowledge or admit he had an addiction. And never once did he ask for help with it. As a result, he died—alone, addicted, angry, and very out of control.

In times of grief and sorrow I will hold you and rock you and take your grief and make it my own. When you cry, I cry and when you hurt, I hurt. And together we will try to hold back the floods to tears and despair and make it through the potholed street of life.

—Nicholas Sparks, *The Notebook*

CHAPTER 11

UNCOMFORTABLE CONVERSATIONS

My youngest son and I are driving to our cousin's house tonight for dinner. We do this weekly now. It's great to see family, get out of the house, and have a nice visit. Since we moved out of California this year, I am feeling the distance of our family and friends. They seem so far away. It was a necessary move after the fires, but it's been an adjustment. The drive is usually the same - listening to music we like and talking about out day. This is normally the time I get the download of the day's events, like the funny videos they saw, what they did or didn't like about school, conversations they had with their friends, and any plans they are making. Tonight, the conversation is a little different. "I wish I remembered more about dad," our youngest son states.

Connor doesn't talk much about his father. Feelings are hard for him to express and often come up spontaneously, in the moment, often unrelated to what he's doing. Adding to that the complexity of a father who died by suicide, and I imagine these are really tough feelings for him to get at. When it happens, deep feelings float to the surface and are suddenly just sitting there, ready to be discussed. I've learned to kind of brace for impact.

Since he turned eleven, Connor's questions have become more specific. They don't come very often, but when they do, they hit hard. They are clear, direct, thought-evoked. He's starting to put things together, like how things will look in the future for him now that he is without a father. He's coming to terms with his father's actions from four years ago and how they play a dramatic part in how his life is today. He now sees what consequences look like because of his father's suicide. In the case of losing his father, the results, he often finds, are not good for him. The outcomes always seem empty. His father is gone. Tonight, the theme of missed opportunities is ready for discussion.

In response to his comment, I start telling him his dad grew up outside New York. I tell him about his grandparents, how they adored his father, how they moved from New York to Florida, how they raised him there, and how he eventually moved to California, which is where we met. I tell our son the stories that his father told me - his family had a house on the water in Massapequa, and his parents loved the water. They always had him in a boat, catching fish, sailing, or digging for clams. The stories about his growing up years are my favorite. For example, whenever they needed him to sleep, they just put him in the boat, turned the engine on, and took him for a spin around the lagoon. He would immediately drift off. I talk about how nice his grandparents sounded and that I am sure they would have adored their grandsons.

The next question catches me by surprise. "Do you think he died by accident or on purpose?" he asks.

"He died on purpose. He planned it," I reply. My stomach goes into knots. The time has come for me to explain the suicide. It's been four years. He's heard this information before, but he's processing it right now.

"He knew that last night that we saw him that he was going to kill himself?" he asked.

I sit there in silence, dumbstruck. I struggle with my answer. This is one of the raw and painful aspects of suicide. This is what makes it stand out. People who suicide often plan the event. It's a harsh reality that is mind-boggling to those left behind. I want to desperately say, "I don't know," and keep the topic of his loss open with mystery. Or maybe, "he just stumbled." Or "he fell and accidentally killed himself." Any answer like that would be so much easier than telling our children their father planned on leaving them. Let my son think innocent things: His father was taken from him. Keep him naive about the dark state his father's mind was in and all bad choices he consciously made leading up to that moment. But the truth is that he planned it. He thought it out, he decided to do it, and he even made goodbye videos. He reconciled it in some twisted way in his mind and then he left, without saying goodbye. The truth is that Tom chose all of it. It's painful to talk about. I am reminded that it's not just about the missing. It's also about the abandonment. In those final acts, their father abandoned his loved ones. All of us. He abandoned every single person who cared about him.

And if we could weigh loss and compare who loses most, I would say our children have suffered the most from his actions, regardless of the reasons. They have felt the weight of his decision in unmeasurable ways. I keep talking, struggling with what to say, and how much to say. I always wonder about what impact the information I relay will have on my children's minds. I worry if I say something, and I worry if I don't say it.

I also struggle with the harsh reality of truth when it comes to suicide. I want to show compassion for their father, explain the suffering. But I also want my son to understand that, even as much as he idolizes his father, killing yourself is hurtful to others. That's one of the messages I want him to hear. There is no excuse or justification that will ever rationalize the actual loss for those left behind.

As I speak with him, there is still some part of me that doesn't want to think about these details or the facets of his death. How desperate Tom must have been to be in that state of mind. How uncomfortable he was. How much pain he was in. And how I was unable to help him. Talking about it makes it so real. "He was very angry and doing drugs, and his mind wasn't working right," I tell him.

"He thought he didn't matter?" my son replies.

"Do you think he mattered?"

"Oh, my gosh, yes," my son says. "He was very important."

"Yes, he was. And he had a lot of people who loved him."

"Do you think the drugs had anything to do with it?" he asks.

"Yes, I think the drugs had a lot to do with it because they helped change the way he was thinking, and he wasn't thinking clearly. He thought he was alone and that no one cared about him. You cared, I cared, his friends cared, his family cared. He had a lot of people who loved him and would have helped him if he had asked."

Silence.

With my stomach still in knots I continue, "He thought we would be better without him, and he was wrong. He had problems like we all do, and we have to learn to work through them. It's one of life's hardest lessons. He probably thought he could get rid of them by dying, but you don't really know if the problems go away or just go with you. You have to work the problems through. And sometimes, you have to ask for help. That's just how it is."

Again, silence. He is looking down at his fingers in his lap. I can tell he is processing this, and it's making him very sad. I'm layering my story with messages I want my son to hear, but I can see that what's really there is a son's broken heart.

Simply broken. Broken trumps logic. I'm sure the sadness was there before, but the answers to the questions aren't helping. There's no way they could. These are the conversations I hate the most. The children deserve answers. They are struggling to understand what their dad did, why other parents don't do this, why their father could do this, why he didn't ask for help, what they could have done, how come their dad had to go, and how they will live life without him.

He asks to change the topic and starts talking about a YouTube video he recently watched. I have tears in my eyes as I keep driving, suddenly taken over by this painful dialogue we entered into. I'm overwhelmed with emotion. The pain of suicide never seems to go away. Another conversation that catches me by surprise. And I hate it. Since Tom's death, I've never had a comfortable conversation about his suicide with anyone. It makes me really uncomfortable. It's a dialogue that has never just flowed with ease. It's always hard, bitter, raw, and awkward.

And it brings up this agony that is so painful. I know the agony is because I am unwilling on some level to reconcile what happened. There is still a part of me that is so resistant to the fact he killed himself and is gone. On some level, it still feels unbearable. I know I'm not alone with this feeling. I'm sitting next to another soul who is also desperately missing Tom. It's agonizing for him. It's unresolved. It's a story left unfinished yet forced to have an ending because he suicided. And that ending has never felt right. I am reminded that my biggest sadness is for our children. I am sitting with our eleven-year-old son, who is still struggling to make sense of what happened to his father. From the specifics of how it happened to how he is now left all alone to deal with it. Without his father there, life feels different for Connor.

Another layer has been added this year, this one is of an eleven-year-old boy who is seeing himself heading into life without his father. A father to spend time with. A father to get to know. A father to be his champion and friend. A father who is alive. And not just any father, *his* father. The father he knew and was taken away from him for no reason that makes sense to him. Nothing could ever really justify that. I get it. Now he's seeing he'll never have that opportunity so many boys have to know his dad and get to spend lots of time with him. He'll never get to tell him about the YouTube videos he makes on his channel or his favorite games on Roblox. He'll never get to share how much he likes Goldfish crackers. They'll never have hamburgers and milkshakes together or see the next *Star Wars* movie together. Or get to read stories with his dad at bedtime, travel to foreign places with him, play pranks on him. The collecting of memories together is over, as is the possibility to hang out with or hug each other ever again. That's huge for this kid. And he is feeling all of it right now. He doesn't say it, but I can see it on his face. It's breaking his heart. It's almost too much to bear. I desperately want to protect him, but I can't shield him from this. It's just too big. All I can do is just be with him and hurt for all of us.

A person who dies by suicide dies a single death while those left behind die a thousand deaths.

—AllianceofHope.org

CHAPTER 12

STILL LEARNING HOW TO LOSE YOU

Years are passing, and the grief still catches me by surprise. Instinctively, I start feeling sad and on the verge of tears. I check the inventory of my life. I look at my schedule, count stressors, find nothing out of the ordinary, and then suddenly, it hits me—grief.

One of those dates is coming up. It's especially rough during the holidays or the anniversary of his death. And then he comes into my awareness. It's Tom. After all these years, it's still about him. I guess, like the lyrics in the Kaitln Doubleday song, "I'm Still Learning How to Lose Him." It's always been about Tom. I spent seventeen years of my life in a relationship with this man. I wish I could say that after all this time, I don't think about him, that I don't miss him, that I've learned how to move on or to compartmentalize the sadness and the space he used to fill in our lives. But it's simply not true. Robin Chodrak wrote, "The only way to resume your life in a healthy way after you have lost someone you loved is first to deeply grieve."

Over the years, my grief over Tom's death has, like Robin's journey, led me to a place of redefining who we are as individuals and as a family without him. With the passing of time, we have learned how to live, how to move in life without him. Around that hole. Around the missing. We move around that experience we had that he was a husband, father, friend, and permanent fixture in our lives but somehow is no longer physically here with us, where he should be. In that space where we planned on him being. Where we needed and wanted him. There is a constant void there. An absence of energy, happiness, sadness, peacefulness, love, memories, expectations, things to still to come. The life and future we had with Tom is now gone. Those things have been sucked into that hole.

"These are the lovely bones that had grown around my absence," Alice Sebold wrote in *The Lovely Bones*. "It happened after I was gone. And I began to see things in a way that let me hold the world without me in it." We hold his lovely bones. We are still learning how to hold them in a world without him in it. We are still learning how to see things in a new way. How to live in this new existence.

There are still regular reminders - a mannerism the boys have that looks just like their dad, a question they had about which *Star Wars* movie he liked, what his favorite meal was, a question about how he and I first met. I keep these moments alive to embed in our children the feeling of family and relationship. Storytelling holds a special place in our family because I am able to capture memories and recreate experiences of our time together before the children and tell a story, his story. I keep a part of him alive in our memories, which the children will carry on in their memories. The stories also become part of their identities, showing them the family, they have been born into. There was some tragedy there, but there was also a lot of love and good memories. Our memories are part of the narrative of our family that I am helping the children weave together. They will need help learning how to tell this part of our family story. It will always be a difficult story to tell.

The kids have often asked about our love story. They love most of the stories I tell about the time Tom and I met. How we met, how we fell in love, how we wanted them as our kids from the moment we declared our love for each other. They ask to hear their birthing stories, particularly those focusing on where their dad was and what he was doing before, during, and after their births. "Oh, yes, he was there," I say. "He didn't miss a moment and would have given birth to both of you if he could have." I tell them we used to joke about that; secretly, I think he was jealous I was the one who could get pregnant and give birth to them. It took two of us all the way. In many ways, Tom was an amazing father. And for that I am grateful.

As our children ask the questions, I see they are still weaving a story of who their father was and how he lived. They need to hear they were in a relationship with him, a big part of his world, that he wanted to be a father, and that it was the number 1 role in his life. They try to integrate the loss caused by not having him in their lives anymore by confirming how much they meant to him. This is a shadow of the loss. They ask about the dark shadow stuff too—how the addiction led to so many bad choices, why he didn't ask for help. Questions will randomly come up sometimes, and I've learned to flinch when I hear them. It's raw, painful material, so I try to be as honest as I can and tell the truth without hurting them in the process. When necessary, I edit those details that don't need to be rehashed. These are not the stories I had planned to tell my children. Not experiences I thought either of us would leave behind as part of our legacies for our family. My truth, his truth, both hold this darkness now. Addiction is a hard legacy, but suicide adds a darker shadow. It would be so much easier to dismiss their questions and offer instead short, contrite answers. Compartmentalize all of it. Defend against it. But I don't.

My maternal instinct dictated initially to shelter them and not talk about the suicide. But I saw them able to put things together, and combined with their memories, they knew something more had happened beyond him just passing. They knew on some deep level that something wasn't right with their father. They did not learn how he died that night. I told them he had health issues so we could just focus on grieving and the loss. Against the counselor's recommendations, I waited three years to tell them the details of his death. My instincts said they had suffered through a divorce, the severing of our family system, and then through his death, and that was enough for them. They would come to me when they were ready to hear more. What I felt we all needed most after his passing was time. Time for things to settle, time for things to heal, time to integrate such a devastating loss, and time for life to move forward. So, I waited. I trusted my instincts and my intuition. And it was one of the best decisions I have ever made. Time really helped them absorb such catastrophic information.

I've learned that dying is not the only big-ticket item for people to contend with, but how someone dies can hold equal weight. Finding out their father committed suicide was devasting for them. It sent a shock wave through our house. They each responded. The first direct question hit me midday, right in the middle of another conversation, three years following his death. I was talking with our oldest about a movie, and suddenly he asked, "Was it a suicide?"

I paused as I felt the shift in our conversation. I remember looking out the window, trying to find the right words. I knew the questions would come someday, so I had prepared something to say. But at that moment, my prepared response escaped me, and the words didn't come out like I thought they would. I answered the questions. "Yes, it was a suicide." Then, "Yes, the suicide was related to the drug use. Yes, he was very unhappy." And finally, "And no, there was nothing you could do about it." Heartbroken, our oldest sobbed, wondering why his father hadn't come to him so he could have helped him. "He chose not to ask for help," I replied. A bitterly disappointing response.

It was not the role model answer either of us was looking for. I remembered back to that day when the coroner told me, "Suicide is a selfish act." And here we were. Not only was it a selfish act, but this father had a son who wanted to help him. A son who would have done anything to help him. I would have never expected such a compassionate response from a child. Let alone our child. What a heart.

I think older brother then mentioned it to younger brother. I chose not to push the topic on him. I waited. And a few weeks later, when our youngest was ready, he asked a couple of questions. He sat quietly for a few minutes, absorbing the responses. Then he said he didn't want to talk about it anymore, and that was that. It took almost a year before he could bring it up again, randomly on a drive to our cousin's house. Over the years, he has asked questions about his father's death, still trying to put the pieces together. Sometimes he will cry, but the moments are rare. I have deep respect for how he grieves. This suicide left both children with a deep sadness, sense of loss, and a suffering that will, unfortunately, never be forgotten.

Over the years, our children have looked to me to see how to respond to an event like this. I have seen them listening and watching me to learn how to deal with it. They take notes on my explanations, my perspectives, my emotional responses. They have felt my tears and sadness. They have felt the power of the stories I tell them. It was as if they were looking for someone to help them make sense of this tragedy because suicide just doesn't make sense. I still feel the children's disappointment and layering the conversations sometimes. I hear it in their voices. I see it in their eyes. It is in those brief pauses when we are talking, and suddenly, they become quiet and gaze off. So much they have to contend with, so much for their little minds to make sense of and grow into. I feel their loss mostly in those quiet moments.

Lately, the questions have been more existential. They ask why we are here on this earth, and why God took him away. Sometimes they resent God. Our oldest no longer believes in a God that could let something like this happen. I get it. It's hard to make sense of. It's just so much disappointment mixed with unmet needs. We talk about how important it is to live and how God has a plan and purpose that we don't always know. And that God will take care of him. I emphasize their father is not alone wherever he is. I pray that he is in a place where he is safe and with his loved ones, getting the help his soul needs to heal. I think in *Temples on the Other Side: How Wisdom from "Beyond the Veil" Can Help You Right Now,* Sylvia Brown description of heaven describes that. I provide answers to our children as best as I can, hoping that these thoughts, explanations, and my support will help to build a bridge of understanding in our children's minds.

Suicide was not the way to healing. That I know. And I think the children know that now also. The circumstances under which he died—the act itself, the response from the world to his death and to a suicide—all say that was not the thing to do. That was not the way to die. I will never forget the state I woke up in that night and how unsettling the experience was. I know from the dark energy left behind in the house that it was not a place of love and healing. It was dark, disturbing energy. After experiencing that firsthand, I would never wish suicide on any human being.

I know that those who suicide often say that they can't go on anymore and that anything would be better than where they are. But I simply disagree. I have a different perspective. I have a different mindset. I know from years of helping people, from seeing little miracles happen over and over, from having a strong faith in something greater than us, from the outside looking in that we create our own hell. I've seen it. And I've seen people turn their lives around. I've seen people dig themselves out of the hole they are in. I've seen people overcome things they never thought they could. I've seen them search the depths of their souls. I've witnessed them fall into an existential abyss and climb back out again. What I know is that we can overcome so much. And there are always other options to suicide.

Your memory feels like home to me.

So whenever my mind wanders, it always finds its way back to you.

—Ranata Suzuki

CHAPTER 13

LIVING IN THE CANYONS OF GRIEF

Today I am cleaning out voice mails on my phone and suddenly see Tom's name. It's at the bottom of the voice mails I saved. Instinctively, I search for his messages and realize this voice mail is the only sound of his voice I have left. Then, like a wave of agony, it hits me that he is gone. Permanently gone. I know the sound of his voice; it's so familiar. It's etched into my memories. I'd recognize his voice anywhere. I hesitate to listen because I know it will make me sad. I do it anyway, in a compulsive way. The same way we morbidly look at accidents when we drive by them. He sounds so close, like he is physically here, just around the corner. But he is gone. This is it. This is all that's left of him. Most of the messages I saved in my voice mails were about the kids. Even while embroiled with a terrible drug addiction, he had tried to stay connected to the children.

I look for the last message he left me before he died. A call is registered on the list but with no message. It shows it at 1:30 a.m. on October 2, 2014. I knew it would be there. I just needed confirmation. I remembered I shot up out of bed as the phone woke me that morning. I knew something was wrong. For a long time, I revisited the memory of that call. For a long time, it haunted me. I should have answered that call. Suicide, love, loss, living, dying are all things you don't simply get over. They remain. In pieces sometimes, sometimes as threads in a fabric, sometimes as remnants. Or as a voice mail.

To traverse this path of complex grief means to settle into deep canyons of grief and loss. You learn to sit with the suffering and the agony. You climb into that spot and stay. You settle in there for long periods of time, nestled in the nooks of the deep walls until it becomes so familiar to you it feels like a part of who you are. Stillness and quietness absorb the sadness and all the misery. Elisabeth Kübler Ross wrote about acceptance as the final stage of grief. There is no real acceptance in this grieving process for me. Instead, remembrance is permanently etched into my soul. Nor is there reconciliation. Both would require compromise, and there is no one on the other side to compromise with because he is dead by his own hand. Gone. Resignation has formed instead with a very heavy heart. Resignation leaves space for the memories to always remain on some level unsettled. The missing never stops; the memories, questions, and pain all become parts of your landscape, slowly being molded from these experiences we call trauma, loss, and tragedy. My landscape now has holes his life was supposed to fill. Instead, there is nothingness there, just emptiness, quietness. Things happen as you move forward that remind you, slowly, that life is still moving on but without him now. Other reminders display the fact that our lives no longer connect and move around each other. We permanently move in different dimensions. Here, as those loved ones left behind, we move around this empty space, always knowing it's there. It is always there. And with it, regular reminders of him bring that moment of unease, of realization, of loss all over again. Again, we stand next to the hole that has the goneness in it. The goneness that should not be there.

My heart aches daily. The sadness always feels just around the corner. I'm used to it. It is part of the suffering that arrived after he suicided. Because he suicided. In *Ambiguity of Suffering,* Nader Shabahangi writes,

> Suffering itself is given a right of citizenship. Over the last centuries, increasingly suffering has been denied this citizenship and has come to be understood as aberrant, devious, and sick … Suffering is a part of the world, part of the human experience. By denying it citizenship, to our detriment, we deny part of a world that co-exists with us and belongs essentially to our constitution.

Suffering has been a part of my landscape for years now. As I suffer, I weave this pain into my narrative of living, into the understanding of what happened and how something like this could have happened. Sometimes I feel the pain that comes with it. Simple broken heartedness, aching sadness. Misery from losing someone in such a terrible way. I absorb the presence of such violence. This terrain is tough, raw, and real. Keep grieving. Stay aware of what the experience of real deep loss is like. Honor the broken heartedness. Grant the suffering citizenship into the canyons where I dwell. Stay with the confusion, the questions, the agony, the not understanding, and all the not knowing. Surrender to it. Accept the heartache. It's permanent now. And as I do that, I feel this release in my soul as I surrender it to God. He can hold it for a while as I send threads of purple velvet ribbons up into the atmosphere. Ribbons upon ribbons, floating up into the vast expanse of the unknown.

Compassionate action starts with seeing. Yourself when you start to make yourself right and when you start to make yourself wrong. At that point you could just contemplate the fact that there is a larger alternative to either of those, a more tender, shaky kind of place where you could live.

—Pema Chodron

CHAPTER 14

SURVIVOR GUILT

I dreamed of Tom last night. This doesn't happen very often, but when it does, the dreams are always unsettling. I'm sure at this point, with this much time passing since his death, they are more about me than him. Jung theorized that our dreams reflected internal conflicts, apropos here. My soul is still trying to reconcile events and feelings, reflecting symbols of internal conflicts I struggle with. In these dreams, I am desperately worried about him. I'm always trying to find him, but I never do.

We are in a huge hospital, waiting to see a doctor to treat one of the boys for an allergy. While in the waiting room, two staff members walk by, and I overhear one mention Tom's name to the other. I immediately turn around to hear what they are saying, wondering if it is him. I follow them and hear the Tom they were talking about has voluntarily checked himself into the psychiatric ward. Instinctively knowing it's him, I get up to go find him. I begin walking and find myself suddenly in a long walkway with multiple corridors full of people. I am not sure which corridor to take.

A nurse approaches me from the middle of the crowd and tells me she is very concerned about him and looking for the right specialist to consult with. She suddenly sees a woman in a red sweater walking toward us. She heads toward her, telling me that is who she needs to consult with, so I follow. As she begins to explain what the situation is, the medical person looks at her, pretending to pay attention, but she is focused on something else. She is blocked, detached, shut off. She doesn't stop but continues walking while the nurse is trying to talk to her. Then she suddenly disappears into the sea of people.

There are more people now. Everywhere. Like a crowded football stadium. They are moving in all directions. Urgently we start to search for her. The nurse keeps telling me how important it is that she get a consult with that specialist. Still unsure of which corridor to take, I struggle to decide if I should stay with the medical person to find the woman in the red sweater or go to the psychiatric unit. I realize I have no idea where it is. I just know I need to get there to help. There is an intense urge, a need to see him and help him. But underneath, I feel such a distance between us. Literally and figuratively. I have so much caring and concern for Tom yet no idea what is going on with him. My instincts are primal and override all decisions: I must help him, and I must reunite the family. I know I can do it.

I stay with the nurse and as we search for the woman in the red sweater, all I see are people walking through the corridors of the hospital. Everyone looks the same. I turn and see the nurse I had been walking with has also now disappeared into the crowd.

Lost and unsure which way to go, I wake up and realize I am where I always am—trapped between that terrible choice of leaving him to take care of the children or staying to help him. I see that I was all the characters in the dream—the worried wife, the scurrying nurse, the detached doctor. My energy is the hordes of people with us in the hallway, scattering in different directions. The hospital and its corridors are the all the choices I had to make with such limited information, with so many unknowns. And I was always unsure which way to go, which decision to make.

This agony has layers to it. It is the fact that I chose my children over helping him. I had to. The agony in me is also from the fact that I would do it again in a heartbeat. I would abandon him to choose my children. And what a terrible choice to have to make. And with that choice, because I chose them, I had to let him go and not help him. On some level, I knew he was struggling; I just didn't know how close to death he was or that suicide was an option he was considering. The agony is in watching a human being get eaten up by drugs and a subsequent crazy mind. There will always be a part of me that wonders what I could have done differently—if I could have actually done anything—and what actions I could have taken to create a different outcome, one where he was still alive. The agony also still sits in the fact that he is gone.

There is a mix of agony and suffering. It's in the fact that he never came to me. He never admitted his addiction, and he never asked for help. That's a painful realization. He never asked me, a trained counselor, of all the people in the world he knew and the one he was closest to, to help him. The counselor in me and the healer both feel disabled by this fact. I knew there were deeper issues he needed to work through. There is also agony in the harsh reality that there was nothing I could do, although my desire and instincts want to dictate otherwise. The rescuer and the narcissist in me both seem able to tolerate that. There is a reality there. The reality is that he had gone to great lengths to push me away and continued to keep me as far away as possible during his decline and engulfing addiction. He was self-destructing. No one was going to save him. And bearing witness to that has been heartbreaking. I suffer in the fact that he, on some level, chose to self-destruct. To see someone you love—the other parent of your children, the partner you knew for so many years—in a state like this is a terrible burden. Agony abounds here. The mother, wife, co-parent, and friend felt blocked when she so wanted to help. Or at least try.

The harsh reality was that the addiction slowly took over our lives and relationship, shifted our family dynamics, and moved me out of his life and away from a position of being able to help him. I made a choice and moved further away from him, moving instead closer to focus and care for our children. I left him alone to flounder with the addiction and subsequent madness that eventually took over. I did not cause the addiction or make the choice for him to use drugs. But I did leave him. Even for the right reasons, I abandoned him at a critical time and left him alone, maneuvering through a very existential space. And that stays with me, to always wonder if things could somehow have played out differently, suffering from the outcome of the choices I had to make. Jung noted that sometimes turning internal conflicts into images alleviates the emotions. I am hoping for that someday.

There is love in holding and there is love in letting go.

—Elizabeth Berg, *The Year of Pleasures*

CHAPTER 15

"IT'S REALLY HARD TO LIVE WITHOUT HIM"

We are having breakfast at a bakery today, a fun treat we do sometimes to change up our homeschool routine. We are looking at the cute teapots and china displayed on the wall, creating a Danish theme. As we sit there, I'm suddenly hit with one of the powerful statements our sons make about losing their father. Out of the blue, my son's eyes are suddenly filled with tears as he says, "It's really hard to live without him." I wonder how sitting in a bakery led to that statement. He starts to continue the thought, but then stops midsentence and looks down at his plate, trying not to cry. The tables next to us are empty, but there are people directly behind him. He's fighting back tears, which brings tears to my eyes. The more stoic and prideful of our two boys, I am stunned this is what is underneath that smile and easygoing nature.

He looks up at me, and our eyes lock, just like they used to when I would drop him off at the bus on the way to school. For a moment, this child is offering something incredibly deep. I stare back and fight the urge to lunge across the table and hug him. I'm grateful for our children and for the love we have for each other. We sit in silence, staring at each other in a rare moment of vulnerability.

The moment passes, and he eventually looks away. These have become the moments that have made us closer as a family. We have bonded through a tragedy that hit our family hard. I begin talking about their father, how he lost his parents back-to-back, first his mother and then his father. "I can't imagine," our son says.

"Neither can I," I reply. In these moments, I am struck by the compassion that is in our son's heart and the deep compassion I feel for my ex-husband. At the age of eleven, his world was torn apart, everything taken away from him, his parents, his home, the life he knew. All gone. No safety: the village wiped out. The loss must have felt insurmountable for him. I explain to our son that sometimes events like that create deep wounds in people. They can make people feel depressed or like they don't want to live anymore. I share my regret that his father chose to turn to drugs to fill the wound instead of going back to counseling and getting help. That act led to him self-destructing, another thread in the legacy narrative that is hard to weave.

"I think he just wanted to be with his parents again," I say to him.

"I get that," he replies.

As I watch our children grow, I repeatedly commit myself to them. I focus on healthy living, being in the relationship, handling emotions, and being fully present in these moments of sadness. They hold expectations and disappointments. My new desires, because of this tragedy, are now to create experiences in our children that reflect a more hospitable world despite this tragic loss. As I pledge to face things with them head-on, I remember that we must focus on living, stay focused on love, on loving each other, and on moving forward. I pray I have the strength, knowledge, and courage to forge ahead on the road now in front of us.

Don't you know yet? It's your light that lights up the world.

—Sufi saying

CHAPTER 16

A HINT OF SOMETHING YOU LEFT BEHIND

I can feel a shift in my mind this year. An emphasis is slowly being placed on remembering. The grieving widow is retreating now. For the past few years, she has been front and center, so present in my everyday living. Now she is resting in the background, and the remembering woman takes the stage. The memory keeper. At times, I feel like I am an old woman sitting in a rocking chair, knitting, and remembering. With one simple task, to remember, to remember something you left behind.

The remembering becomes an important piece in the grief process and in managing the immensity of the loss. It definitely serves a purpose. The lack of his presence was so intolerable for such a long time. That surprised me, considering how much conflict we had between us at the time of his death. I honestly thought I would not have such an emotional response to his death. I clearly underestimated the depth of love, relationship and attachment. Years of experiences, feelings, and memories piled up, hoarded into the recesses of my mind. All suddenly unloading with his death. Exposed now, raw and painful.

Remembering has helped with time, to move me to this new place of finding the real feelings I had for him buried underneath. And it has helped me to learn how to be OK with being left with nothing but memories. I feel a strong urge to remember. All of it. In whatever shape or form it comes. Him, our time together, the kids, our family, the house, the vacations, the conflicts, the dogs, the job changes, the divorce, the storyline, the suicide, the events that happened after it. Remembering is of the upmost importance now. I can't forget; to do so will mean I have forgotten him and our lives together.

There is guilt that comes with thoughts pushing to keep him alive in my mind. I know I can start to let go now, but in some ways, I can't. It keeps us in a relationship because regardless of the passing of time, I see some part of me still not ready to let him go. There is still a part of me that cannot tolerate him being gone. There is an unbearableness that comes with tragedy. No one tells you that. A perpetual intolerance, an unbelievability, and a permanent inability to accept it.

So remembering takes its place. Remembering can take up a lot of mind space, partially because I'm still trying to find memories to add to the timeline of our lives together. I'm still weaving our stories together for our children. It also helps in creating a timeline and story that make sense to me. I'm still looking for reconciliation, for forgiveness, wondering if there will ever be an outcome in this process of searching. We have been taught that laying things to rest is a good thing. Stop thinking about it, put it away, and move forward. Move on. This event has never been laid to rest for me. And now I don't think it ever will. I'm still learning how to live without him, how to live with the fact that he suicided. I see now that those facts will always unsettle me. His suicide has never felt right and never will. That is my truth. I can accept that he committed suicide and that he chose that, but I'm not OK with his passing on in that manner because the implications and the outcomes were profound.

In many cases, suicide reflects a giving up and an unspoken agony. It reflects an intolerance, whether in the form of an inability to accept something, a perception that a person can't handle living, or the inability to handle pain associated with living. Perhaps a person is raging and retaliating or seeking it as an ending for some other reason. Those facts remain unresolved when a person suicides. They suicided for a reason. And the reason is often where the work is, not in the act of suicide. The only time I would argue the opposite would be in assisted suicide, euthanasia. Tom died in the middle of doing his work, and the work was abruptly stopped. It remains unfinished. As a result, his life has gone unfulfilled. Stopped abruptly, midstream, midlife. And I don't think that will ever be OK with me.

I now see that memories are the only real things I have left of him, so I have to get it right. It feels like assembling a big history book, filling in sections, finding old pictures, telling new stories. It's all a part of the blanket I have been weaving, this narrative with the tapestry of colors and experiences blending together more comfortably now.

The other part of the remembering is about how to keep him alive in our world, which has become a new life without him in it. There's a permanency there. He has been exiled into the depths of our consciousnesses, never to be seen again. And so the tapestry continues to be woven, the history book created. Every time I think I am finished and can lay it to rest as a finished work, a new thread comes up asking to be added, or a new image appears.

Stephen Jenkinson talks about "the skill of broken heartedness." Broken heartedness is a theme here. I feel like it easily goes unnoticed or is marginalized in our culture. Get over it, move on. But I argue that is not the thing to do. Broken heartedness is really important. I feel the impact that this loss has had on my being in the saddest way possible. It's so easy to remember the good times, the niceness of a person, the loving moments, the laughter, the person's good side. It's much harder to remember the dark stuff, the ugliness, the pain, the guilt, the unanswered, what you can't reconcile, what can't be undone, what can't be forgiven. How do you honor such a complex process? And how do you honor the complexity of being human? The loss and grief have to be part of this weave. They have to be acknowledged and integrated. The darkness, like dark colors, must be woven into the tapestry. Suffering must also sit at the table. It must be included in the storytelling and in the images. When the stories are remembered, when the memories are brought back, the grieving widow is acknowledged ever so briefly, and the loss fulfills its rightful place. More threads are woven into the narrative of our family history. Ugly threads, perhaps, but still threads. Release, weave, release, weave. Rest. Breathe.

How do we deal with broken heartedness? What do we say? How long do we grieve? How many tears do we shed? This type of death brings with it an unwelcome broken heartedness that can last a lifetime. It makes the tapestry thick and complicated to weave. The agony creates a painful ache. It's a vulnerability that is hard to talk about and hard to feel, like needling with a strained hand throbbing from pain. No one deserves to lose a loved one, but when it has the possibility of being something that was preventable, when you think about how tragically the person died, when you sit with the shock of it and the pain of how unhappy he or she was, combined with the permanence of the loved one being gone, there is added misery. Tragedies create broken heartedness. Harder threads to weave, tough, stubborn, and ugly. Like getting pricked by the needle with every stich. Weave, prick, release. Weave, prick, release.

My broken heartedness includes the unfinished plan I had mapped out in my mind that he would be around for a long time. I know it sounds simple, but I thought he would be around for years. Decades. I was sure he would live into old age. Even in the depths of his addiction, I was sure that he would get himself out of it. He would be OK. Because it was Tom, and he always landed on his feet. He was a survivor. He would get back on track, back to the way I had known him for so many years—strong and resilient. I see now that those were wishful thoughts floating through a mind filled with good intentions.

My broken heartedness sits in the unexpected outcome of a sudden death. He and I were the youngest of our generation. With four generations on both sides of our families, we were in the middle, not the youngest or the oldest, but the youngest of the next generation to eventually be the oldest. He and I, in my mind, sat in the position of seeing many family members pass. We would be attending our share of funerals. His funeral was never a part of that scenario because we were younger. I secured a place of longevity in my timeline for both of us. I secured that. And I counted on it. That's how things were supposed to happen. Even divorced, there was a security there for me, knowing we would both be around for a long time simply because he was so dedicated to our children. I could rest assured that the boys would always have two parents, no matter what was happening between Tom and me. In some way, I depended on that. I needed that. We would always have someone there for the children. Together we would make it work. We had a plan with a backup plan embedded into it.

When he died, I scrambled to make sense of things. He didn't live a long life. I no longer had a co-parent to help raise the children. Our family system had been handicapped further. And as for plans? Things turned out so differently than I had expected. Now what plans should I make? My security in my plans let me down. One of the surest things I felt in this life was gone. I sometimes now feel like I'm treading through life more cautiously, being careful not to tip the balance. Don't make that choice; do this instead. Wait, don't make a decision on that. Hold that thought. I could be wrong now, so I'll get back to you on that. Sometimes I am unable to commit. Other times, I am unable to decide. Sometimes I'm just waiting for the other shoe to drop because now I see bad things can happen.

Was he doing a birth/rebirth thing? Is that what this was about? Was he forced by some cosmic force to suicide as part of a karmic cycle? That would explain how he was taken out of this life so abruptly. Not that this explanation could possibly make sense to a broken heart. And how could that possibly help him? I feel superstitious looking for explanations that don't seem to make sense to me. What if something else equally terrible happens? I tell myself I'll be prepared. Somehow, I'll be able to handle the next tragedy that hits us with better response time, better logic, and with more strength. In the meantime, I'll make better choices. Or I just won't choose at all. I'll avoid it altogether. Perhaps I'll see the next bad thing coming and jump ahead to prevent it. Or I'll respond better to create a different outcome, a better outcome. Things will make more sense next time. I'll know what to look for and how to respond, so I won't be caught so off-guard next time. Next time.

When Victor called, it had been so long since we had spoken, I figured he was calling to relay the bad news that someone had died. He laughed at my concern. He explained he had some of my father's work, boxed up and ready to send. He heard my groan and laughed again. One more box of his writings and work. More things left behind.

Victor was cleaning out his office, returning items to their rightful owners, my father's estate in this case. He was good like that. In the middle of explaining, he asked, "How are you?"

"Oh, we're all good," I said, in that trained response kind of way. I could have answered differently, and perhaps we would have dropped down into an existential space. But that day, I did not tell him my existential thoughts. He was calling about how best to continue supporting the writings of an existentialist. The pragmatics about what to do with unsold written works. As a friend and student of my father, Victor was part of a small community that showed up during the passing of my parents. And I have an immense amount of respect for that. Showing up when it really mattered was where he dwelled. First for my father. When hospice was called in, I'd come over to the house and see Victor sitting on the sofa, waiting. Waiting to help my mother, waiting to sit with my father, waiting to offer support. I remember trying not to cry in front of him and thinking how silly that was, trying not to cry in front of a psychotherapist. What I really wanted to do was break down and sob in his arms, but I responded dutifully instead. To not make it about me. Victor was saying goodbye to my father, and we needed to be there for my mother. I was heartbroken, and he knew it. I was losing one of my favorite people. I think we both were.

We took turns sitting with my father during those last days, always having someone near him while his life was broken down to moments of breathing and living. Pneumonia, "An old person's friend," the doctor called it. Lungs filled, turn him on his side, clean out his throat, still labored breathing, inject morphine. Bring in the hospital bed, provide regular morphine; make him as comfortable as possible. "Yes, I'm sure he can still hear you even though he no longer opens his eyes or speaks." We sat with him, every day while the hospice nurses took turns with my mother at night. Victor was always there. So was Nader. The day I left the room and Nader entered, my father took that opportunity—that one minute of transition, that one moment when he was alone—to pass on. He couldn't do it or wouldn't do it with me or my mother in the room, so he let go with Nader, the person in the house that day who would honor his leaving in that moment without an emotional attachment.

The owner of an assisted-living community, Nader had been there for many people's passings. That's what he did; he honored the living by creating a safe place where they could die with dignity and respect. Nader would not hold on to him or beg him to stay. He walked out of the room to find me in the kitchen. "I think your father just died. I think he's gone."

"He couldn't have," I said in my denial. "I was just in there." Literally twenty feet away, around the corner. Then I remembered the phone had suddenly gone dead. My mother had been trying to fix the phone to finish her conversation. His soul was passing. It was time.

There, strong, calm, gentle, loving. Respectful. Heartfelt. Filling heart space. The things that mattered. The people in your life showing up when it mattered most.

Then again for my mother, just months later. Fewer people around with her passing. She waited until I was there, back at the house next to her, eyes closed, unable to speak, holding her hand to pass on. I had run home that day literally to shower and change clothes. And as I draped the towel over me, the phone rang. "She's passing and asking for you. You need to come."

"I need to get dressed."

"Karen, she's passing. Come now, come now," the caregiver relayed urgently.

I loved that caregiver. She had initially spoken to my mother in a loud, kind of condescending voice when she first arrived, explaining everything she was doing in a slow, loud, methodical manner. My mother finally reached over, gently touched her arm, and said, "My daughter doesn't yell at me or treat me like an idiot." There were no more loud voices after that. Instead, there were soft, gentle tones. Whispers sometimes.

I raced over, hair wet, dry clothes, suddenly at the house again. I had gone home to take a nap, take a break. Sleep when you can, but never the priority. I hadn't been sleeping that well anyway, so I didn't sleep. Instead, I was there by her side, holding her beautiful hands, tears streaming down my face. She felt my hand, and then she took her last breath. She looked so at peace. When I envisioned her death, I saw her in a canoe, heading upstream. She had been saying she wanted my father there when she died, but I never saw him.

There was something profound in the aloneness of my mother's passing. Something she needed to address, ever so briefly. I knew he was there, but just not where I could see him. Ultimately, she was never alone with me and the family on one side, and my father, her parents and her grandparents on the other. Maybe the journey of passing on was the reminder for her that we really aren't alone. Maybe to remind her that the grace of God shines down upon all of us, even at the moment of our passing, when we feel most alone.

Again, Victor was there, so I would not tell him what I was actually thinking. "Help me figure this life thing out, Victor. Tom suicided. Life doesn't always make sense anymore. It's been years, and it still doesn't make sense. After all this time, I still have broken heartedness in me. Experts say it can last a lifetime. What do I do with that? And how do I let go and still honor him? I don't want to forget him."

I kick myself as I realize that I should have asked about his children. In those few moments of connecting, I should have asked about the ones he loved the most, his wife and children. I'm reminded that he and I are both doing our dutiful jobs, briefly relating, simply relating in those moments when the box needs to get shipped out. Another box. Another memory. From another time passed. "We're all shipping out, Victor," I want to say. "Just not today. In the meantime, I'll give you my address, and you can send the box here. Thanks, Victor."

"OK, you too. Take care. Bye."

To live in hearts we leave behind is not to die.

—Thomas Campbell

CHAPTER 17

OPENING THE WINDOWS OF OUR PASTS

Today I'm trying to remember one of the last conversations I had with Tom. Not that it really matters, but I can't remember any. And it bothers me. How could I not have a memory of that? I think more about it. I start to feel desperate, trying to find the details of our last connection. Sometimes things like this seep into my mind, and I'm filled with a mental sort of frenzy, trying to remember, rummaging through anything that will help me make a connection. I look through my phone history and see that I have a voice mail in my messages from the week before. Seven days went by, and those days were his last on this earth. So much happened that week. I wonder what that was like for him. Had he already decided he was going to die? Did he set a day and time? Did he call his sister? Did he say goodbye to his best friend? He must have spent time planning. How long did he know he was going to kill himself?

As I fall back down into this rabbit hole of missed connections, questions, and blurred memories, I realize that while the kids were at school and I was at work, he was preparing to kill himself. He knew he was leaving. It is hard to fathom that he was actively seeking to end his life. Boy, this is dark, ugly stuff. Did he ever want to talk to me about it? Did he ever realize that it was not the right choice? Did he have an awareness of what this would do to his children? Is there anything here I can hold to make sense out of this?

The not-so-great details are painful and surreal to relive. This is how, as a survivor from a loss like this, I put the pieces together, in moments like this. This is what happens with trauma. Moments are reviewed, and sometimes the revisiting breaks new ground, helping to provide a brief feeling of cohesiveness.

In this case, it's connecting the dots for me. He knew he was going to kill himself, and he talked to us without ever saying a word. Never a warning, no real explanation, all while planning it. *And then he told the children he would see them the next day. Denial perhaps, or intentionally misleading? Was he intentionally making their last interaction seem normal by giving them hope, something to look forward to?* Another painful thought. Instead, it backfired, and hope was replaced with suffering. I don't think he intended that.

I go further down the rabbit hole of questions. How many times had he misled us? How many times had he said things that were untrue? As I struggle to remember our last connections and wonder about his state of mind, as always, I come back to the children. *Oh my God, the children. How could he do this to them*?

These are the moments when the windows of my past blow open, and I'm flooded with images and memories. They come out of nowhere and start flying around as I try to catch as many as I can just to remember him. I look for moments that will surprise me, ones that I can hang on to, ones that bring fond memories, or ones that help makes sense of things for me. With them comes a feeling that as time goes by, with each passing year, he becomes more of a memory, a thing from a distant past rather than the person who was just with us. As I am left behind still trying to figure things out, somehow make sense of it, I also see he is no longer real, no longer in the here and now.

Over these past few years, Tom has gone from feeling like an actual person, a living and breathing individual, to what sometimes now feels like just a series of images in my mind. Describing a loss like this seems so superfluous and impossible to put into words. It's a minimalistic attempt, writing simplified words on a page to describe a vast, unexplainable expanse of a relationship. Of years together as a family with memories, experiences, and so many moments. The words can't possibly express the depths of these canyons. It is impossible to cover years in detail on a written page. Sometimes it feels as if he has somehow become nothing more than a line of thoughts, series of memories, and stories all bundled together. The feelings connected to many of these images are still strong because his being filled my heart space. But in reality, he is nothing more than a memory now. A memory that I keep alive. A piece of all our pasts slowly fading, with distance as the driver.

It's been a difficult road to figure out how to weave the narrative of his suicide into my narrative of living. And into our family narrative. Sometimes it feels like a cold wind howling outside the house, reminding me of scary things—the things we can't foresee, the things that go bump in the night. The things that are forever unresolved, unanswered questions, things that don't make sense, mental chaos. All with strong feelings of pain, anger, and sadness.

I am forever wondering how much emphasis to put on his suicide, how much importance to place on it, how descriptive to be, how much to remember him, how many specifics to hold on to. I wonder how much influence it really has versus my perception of how it has truly influenced me. I try on the idea that I could have shut my emotions down and compartmentalized it. I could have let memories become forgotten; I could have been unfeeling. And I am aware that had I done that, I would have been shut off from a deeper part of myself. It would have become a cordoned area of my soul I was never allowed to access. I owe him a lot. His violent death has transformed my soul in some ways and has helped me deepen the relationship I have with myself and with our children. I am grateful for the grief and suffering too.

The longest amount of time I have ever felt introspection has been over the years since he died. I've dug under layers and found things, discoveries that have helped me make sense of me, of him, and of us. I do feel solid within this universe, even without understanding things or knowing the answers. I know our relationship, our family, and our purpose for being. The ground is getting solid again for me.

As I look outside myself and through the windows of this story, the structure of this suicide story is more cohesive now. Looking in one window, I see that I understand our marriage better because it is within the context of a drug addiction. I see the intricate details, especially of the consequences of important words left out, like admitting the addiction. Profound, life-changing words missing. I see mental illness in another window, with the theme of depression and wanting to die. More missing words and an inability or unwillingness to ask for help. I see in another window moments that should have been filled with intimacy, caring, and connection passed in silence instead. I see the burdens we struggled to hold on to while trying to take care of ourselves and each other. In another window, I see deep loss, misery, and suffering related to this attachment and this tragedy. I understand the expanse of that landscape. That mountain range goes on for miles. There are permanent dark clouds in the distance, the result of what suicide leaves in its wake. In another window, I see the impact the addiction itself had on the failure of our family system much more clearly, like stepping-stones lined up across a riverbed. I see us jumping, ever so carefully trying not to tip the balance. I see in another window where the addiction started and how much more destructive it was than I originally thought. Over a period of years, that little creek turned into a rapid, torrid river, taking everything in its path and flooding the surrounding areas.

I contend with moments when I felt inactive and perhaps should have been in action, times when he was in action and should have been quiet and still. I look through those windows sometimes and see scenarios where I should have intervened but held back. Moments when I should have called him out, taken a stand, confronted him. And I look through the window that holds moments he should have come forward and asked for help. That window has many panes in it. There were so many times when he had a choice and chose not to step forward and face his demons in the right way.

His choice stands as a beacon, a reminder that this is not all on my shoulders to carry. We carry this together, regardless of where he is now. I know he can feel all of this. When the winds start to blow, I feel the intolerableness of losing my ex-husband. That in itself is deep, a thread that is woven into all areas of our lives and our story, along with the thread of miserableness. His actions had sweeping consequences, creating threads I did not expect to weave, stories I never thought I'd tell. With the grace of forgiveness, time has let me become OK with my mistakes—all the things I missed as I shake off more of the could haves or should haves. I see I'm still learning to forgive him. Still learning how to let go. I move back and forth between compassion, empathy, and judgment. Resilience is in the middle of it. Sometimes I don't know where to stand on issues or events. The guilt is still there, on some level, forever rearing its ugly head. Just less now.

Resignation still sits where reconciliation should be. But for the first time in years, there is a glimmer of reconstruction. Not for Tom or for losing him, but for God. On a deep level, I find I have been angry and confused that God would allow a world where something terrible like this could happen. And then leave a situation with so many unanswered questions and unmet needs. And a situation that would hurt our children so deeply. I still don't get it. It's such a terrible thing. How could that be? There's silence for answers, the sounds of crickets in place of where there should be answers. I'm learning how to surrender to not understanding. I have to learn to be OK with that. I know now that I will always have feelings about Tom dying, especially in such an angry, violent, and tragic way. On some level, I will always suffer, and I'm OK with that now. That thread has been intricately woven.

Tom's energy has become things that we remember from the past—his likes; the sayings he used; the clothes he wore; his favorite foods, holidays, and traditions; the things he would talk about. He is like a statue, permanently embedded in our psyches now, just not able to interact with us or give us the love we needed from him or receive the love we so wanted to give him. We no longer celebrate living together but share a new type of existence in memory space, looking through the windows of our pasts.

At this point in the grief process, the boys have learned that they can survive without their father. I sensed for a while that they were unsure. Not if they would survive, but *how* they could want to live and justify that after losing their father. A kind of survivor guilt, I think. I'm sure it felt like an impossible task. For them, an impossible event followed by an impossible task—lose your loved one, one of your favorite people in the whole world, one of the key figures in your life, one that you depended on and needed, and then figure out a way to go on. Oh, and be OK with going on in life without him. And be OK with never seeing or hugging him again. There is still an element of unfairness I feel within them. They wonder why them, why their father?

I have chosen not to lose faith. Right now, God and I are just having a disagreement, and I'm still confused and not happy about the outcome. But I know he is still there, and there is something really wonderful and much greater than our humanness. I still look on in amazement at honeybees and hummingbirds, both defying gravity and yet still flying around. I gaze in admiration at giant elephants trudging through miles of landscape. I look in awe at miles of open ocean along the Oregon coast or layers of mountains and forests of the Pacific Northwest. I wonder at the blossom of a single rose blooming in the morning dew and hearing the wind rustle the leaves of the towering trees in our backyard. I watch in awe hundreds of birds fly in a V formation in the sky above over and over again. I listen for our neighbor's child's hysterical laughter. I marvel as thousands of people unify to march or pray. I still smile at the little girl on YouTube making pizza with her dad. I ogle over puppies and still coo at babies. We have kittens in our home, so I sit admiringly as they purr endlessly in my arms. I wonder what is happening in their little minds.

And I see our beautiful boys slowly turning into young men right before my eyes. Our youngest, with his father's long lanky legs, is now well over six feet tall, has rounded shoulders and long hair. Our oldest, setting his ship's course to conquer the vast world out there, is barely able to wait to see it. I hope both our children will know that the experience that love is one of the most important things in this life and that they know how deeply loved they are. I hope they never lose their sense of awe and wonder.

Everything you love will probably be lost but, in the end, love will return in another way.

—Franz Kafka

EPILOGUE

A QUIET SPACE

"Do you know how much I love you?" I asked my son one day.

"No," my son replied. "Tell me."

"I love you as high as the sky and as deep as the ocean, and to infinity. I love you so much it hurts!"

"Well then, you shouldn't love me."

"But I do."

Tickling and giggling ensue.

Those were the same words that Tom and I said to each other for years. Here I was quoting him to his son, using the same words his mother said to him: "As high as the sky and as deep as the ocean." And it hurt. That's the paradox of love. You take a risk, you open yourself up, and in return, you risk getting hurt. And sometimes you do. It's a terrible deal, really, to open your heart, make yourself vulnerable, and then get injured. I wonder who thought that up.

Over these past years, I have worked exceptionally hard to make sure our children know how much I love them, and that others love them. I have worked hard to make sure they keep alive the memory of their father, and to make sure they know their father loved them more than anything. And in a struggle, hurt himself in a way he should not have. I don't have to tell them it hurts because they know that already. They know someone they loved left them. They know drugs hurt him and that suicide took him away from them. And they know they have survived this hardship. They know love hurts. Still, we have to go on. We have to risk loving. We risk hurting. They know that in those moments, we risk everything because we are vulnerable and simple mortals. No superheroes here.

When I look back at moments in my life, at the risks I have taken, loving Tom was the most beautiful risk I ever took. And I would do it again in a heartbeat. I would risk everything to love him again the way we loved each other. And now, risking everything all over again, I raucously love my children, our children, our family, and life. OK, and our cats. As Trudy Carlson describes Satyagraha, we choose to live, to embrace life, and to "Bring joy back into life by appreciating what you have." We hug, we tickle, we laugh, we fight, we disappoint, and we deny. We put off the inevitable, that someday I will pass on. Someday they will lose me, the forever parent. But not today. That can wait. Today we will love until it hurts. "Satyagraha is the wisdom that life is a mixture of suffering and joy."

Our lives are starting to fill out in this new phase of our lives. It's beginning to feel natural now, natural to forge a new existence without him here. There's a quiet space where he used to be. All the times we imagined him in our lives are now dreams of something and someone long gone. We hang on to the memories of the past to confirm and catalogue his existence. I spend time with each of the boys, looking at pictures of their father, sometimes telling stories, talking about important events in our lives. Out of the blue our oldest asked about Tom's parents recently, so I showed him the pictures we have. I shared the photo albums I have been putting together as memories of our families represented in little square images. There is a special album of their father—Tom as a baby, Tom as a little boy, Tom dressed up as Dracula for one of his favorite Halloweens. Tom, at the age of three, with a beautiful head of curls, sitting in red shorts and a cream cardigan on the porch steps. And another one sitting in his mother's lap, smiling up at her, sitting next to his father, who looks lovingly down at him. Then as a young business professional in a suit and tie. Hugging his nephews, smiling with his sister. His life. His memories. His being. Our son loved it. He jumped onto the internet and began looking up Atkinson family ancestry, actively tying the narratives together. That is what we do. We create our narratives of living, and it includes our history.

I do feel afraid sometimes that we will forget him. And that doesn't seem right. As much as I want to help people by writing this book, there is also an internal agenda at play. Some of my fears are driving me to write this. The thoughts go something like, *If I don't write about him, the importance of his existence and his legacy will be lost. His story will be gone forever.* Some days I want to scream at the world, "He was here.

He was a big part of our lives. How dare you forget him." I want to hear it echo through the canyons and across the plains. I want to smash my fists, like the Incredible Hulk, in the Grand Canyon. I want those giant cracks in the canyon walls as a permanent reminder he was here. He existed, he mattered, and he had a terrible ending. And we have suffered with him being gone. In my mind, there is still a space that holds so much. It's of someone who was supposed to be in that space but isn't. There's still a void. It's also a space that holds everything that happened—all the good, the bad, the unreconciled, the acceptance, the resignation, the sadness, the grief, the unbearableness, the determination, the courage, the wondering, the surviving, the forgiveness, and the missing. It's all there, settling in.

The silence I carry with me plays out in my life in various ways. There are days when all I can do is be alone or be outside. I read more. I write more. I seek quality time with our children. I hold them tight more, tell them how grateful I am for them and how much I love them. Love has been a theme of healing in our home. I am grateful for it. And I am grateful for them. I enjoy being alone more, not encumbered by relationships. The grief still comes up at unexpected times. It settles like a little creek that forms after the rain, running through the backyard. Sometimes it dries up; sometimes it trickles like background noise in the landscape of my life. The flooding river is no longer there. The waters have finally receded.

Tom was the love of my life. He was one of the best things that ever happened to me. He was one of the most important things in my life for a long time. Nothing about him can be easily replaced, compartmentalized, or forgotten. He is the father to our children I am now raising without him.

At this stage of our lives, everything feels like we are where we should be. They see and feel how the world is without him now. I know on some level they will never be OK with that. Our youngest son recently said, "I wonder what Dad would be doing if he were here," as if he were standing in the room with us.

"What do you think he would be doing?" I asked.

"What he always does, being nearby, talking on the phone, and working."

Like a story theme in a science fiction novel, his death is like a disruption in the timeline. They will always miss him. They feel the void. He is permanently etched into their beings and their hearts. He still fills heart space. A lot of it. This loss has become part of their narratives in this life. And they are learning to be OK with that.

I teach them what I can: Be nice to yourself, be kind to other human beings, chose good friends, learn self-care, develop a relationship with God, be aware that there is something so much greater than all of us out there. I teach them skills to handle stress, better ways to communicate, how to access feelings of overwhelm, how to manage emotions, and how to ask for help. How to forgive, how to reconcile, and what compassion for ourselves and others looks like. We talk about anger and the power of feelings, including frustration and intolerance. We talk about patience, how to listen, how to problem solve, how to look at choices. I teach them that they always have options. They are learning how to self-direct, how to self-manage, and how to self-regulate. They are learning how to access the courage and determination they have inside.

And they are learning, every day, that they matter. That what they do counts. That they can make a difference. That their actions have consequences. On some primal level, I can feel that their hearts have reconciled with their minds to keep living without him because they have me, and because that's what we do as human beings. Don't step away from this fight, ever. Don't act recklessly or impulsively to hurt yourself or others. They know they are loved and that it's their duty to go on, to keep living, to give and receive the love they so deserve. Together we will make plans and hang the tapestry proudly on the wall as a reflection of our story here, someday to be ancestors.

BIBLIOGRAPHY

Alighieri, Dante. (2017) *Inferno: First Part of Divine Comedy.* Eternal Sun books.

Alliance of Hope for Suicide Survivors (2021). https://allianceofhope.org.

Bolby, John. *Attachment and Loss.* Vol. I, 2nd Ed. New York: Basic Books, 1982.

Bolby, John. *Loss: Sadness and Depression*, Vol. III. New York: Basic Books, 1980.

Brown, Brene. *Braving the Wilderness: The Quest for True Belonging and the Courage to Stand Alone.* New York: Penguin Random House, 2016.

Brown, Sylvia. (2008) *Temples on the Other Side: How Wisdom from "Beyond the Veil" Can Help You Right Now.* Hay House.

Carlson, Trudy. *Suicide Survivor's Handbook.* Benline Press, 2000.

Casey, Nell. *Unholy ghost: Writers on Depression.* New York: Harper Perennial, 1971.

Chodron, Pema. *When Things Fall Apart: Heart Advice for Difficult Times.* Boulder: Shambhala Press, 2016.

Curtin, S.C., Warner, M.A., & Hedegaard, H. Increase in Suicides in the United States, 1999-2014. Center for Disease Control. April, 2016. https://www.cdc.gov/nchs/fastats/suicide.htm

Chodak, Robin. (2017). *Be Gentle with Me, I'm Grieving.* Robin Chodak, 2017. www.robinchodak.com.

Coleman, Graham. *The Tibetan Book of the Dead. First Complete Translation.* London: Penguin Books, 2005.

Curtin, C. C., M. Warner, & H. Hedegaard (2016). *Increase in Suicide in the United States.* NCHS Data Brief #241, 1999-2004. https://www.cdc.gov/nchs/data/databriefs/db241.pdf.

Falke, Ken., & Goldberg, Josh. *Struggle Well: Thriving in the Aftermath of Trauma.* Carson City: Lioncrest, 2018.

Fine, Carla. *No Time to Say Goodbye: Surviving the Suicide of a Loved One.* New York: Broadway Books, 1999.

Frankl, Victor. *Man's Search for Meaning.* Boston: Beacon Press, 1946.

Harlow, H. F., M. K. Harlow, & S. J. Suomi. From thought to therapy lessons from a primate laboratory. *American Scientist* 59, no. 5 (1971): 538–549.

Herman, Judith. *Trauma and Recovery: The Aftermath of Violence—from Domestic Abuse to Political Terror.* New York: Basic Books, 1992.

Hill, F. What it's like to visit an existential therapist. *The Atlantic Weekly.* 2019. Retrieved from https://www.theatlantic.com/health/archive/2019/01/existential-therapy-you-can-ask-big-questions/579292/

Jenkinson, Stephen. *Die Wise: A Manifesto for Sanity and Soul.* Berkeley: North Atlantic Books, 2015.

Jung, Carl. *Man, and His Symbols.* London: Random House, 1964.

Kendrick, Alex. *The Love Dare.* Nashville: B&H Publishing Group, 2008.

Kushner, D. Understand your dreams by using Jung's "active imagination." *Psychology Today, 2016.* https://www.psychologytoday.com/us/blog/transcending-the-past/201610/understand-your-dreams-using-jungs-active-imagination.

Levi-Belz, Y. With a little help from my friends: A follow-up study on the contribution of interpersonal characteristics to post traumatic growth among suicide-loss survivors. *Psychological Trauma: Theory, Research, Practice and Policy* 11(8): 895–904.

Maslow, Abraham. *A Theory of Human Motivation.* Mansfield Center: Simon & Schuster, 1943.

Mayo Clinic. *Complicated Grief. 2020.* https://www.mayoclinic.org/diseases-conditions/complicated-grief/symptoms-causes/syc-20360374.

Mind for Better Mental Health. *Post-Traumatic Stress Disorder.* 2021. https://www.mind.org.uk/information-support/types-of-mental-health-problems/post-traumatic-stress-disorder-ptsd-and-complex-ptsd/symptoms/.

Noel, Brook., & Blair, Pamela. *I Wasn't Ready to Say Goodbye: Surviving, Coping & Healing after the Sudden Death of a Loved One.* Naperville: Sourcebooks Inc, 2008.

Pipher, Mary. *Letters to a Young Therapist, Stories of Hope and Healing.* New York: Basic Books, 2003.

Prigerson, H. G., P. K. Maciejewski, C. F. Reynolds III, A. J. Bierhals, J. T. Newsom, A. Fasiczka, E. Frank, J. Doman, & M. Miller. *Inventory of Complicated Grief: A Scale to Measure Maladaptive Symptoms of Loss.* (1994). Elsevier Science Ireland Ltd. SSDI 0165-1781(95)02757-N. https://endoflife.weill.cornell.edu/sites/default/files/icg_publication.pdf.

Redfield Jamison, Kay. *Night Falls Fast: Understanding Suicide.* New York: Vintage Books, Random House Inc, 1999.

Requarth, Margot. *After a Parent's Suicide: Helping Children Heal.* Sebastopol: Healing Hearts Press, 2008.

Roe, G. Ten Spiritual Truths about Loss and Healing. https://www.beliefnet.com/love-family/life-events/10-spiritual-truths-about-loss-and-healing.aspx?fbclid=IwAR2FHIwqUdKaVvDaUx0mf8dhMjwmNepjgWHkvMXft1b5ez5UprJ13g1PXag

Roe, Gary. *Grief Walk: Experiencing God After the Loss of a Loved One.* Gary Roe, 2020.

Ross, Elizabeth. Kubler. *On Death and Dying: What the Dying Have to Teach Doctors, Nurses, Clergy and Their Own Families.* New York: Macmillan Publishing Company, 1969.

Rumi. Goodreads.com. https://www.goodreads.com/quotes/723832-you-have-to-keep-breaking-your-heart-until-it-opens.

Sebold, Alice. *The Lovely Bones.* New York: Hatchett Book Group, 2002.

Shabahangi, R. *Ambiguity of Suffering.* San Francisco: Elder Academy Press, 2014.

Simmons, Rachel. Odd Girl Out: The Hidden Culture of Aggression in Girls. New York: Houghton Mifflin Harcourt, 2002.

Walker, Pete. *Complex PTSD: From Surviving to Thriving.* Azure Coyote Publishing, 2014. Openlibrary.org

Wilson, Tim, director. *Griefwalker.* National Film Board of Toronto. 2008. 70 minutes.

Wolfelt, A. *Understanding Your Suicide Grief: Ten Essential Touchstones for Finding Hope and Healing Your Heart.* Fort Collins: Companion Press, 2009.

Freedom Pact. "Dr. Irvin Yalom: How to Overcome the Fear of Death", YouTube video, April 1, 2021. https://www.youtube.com/watch?v=iEPFnwYQLkQ

Young-Bruehl, Elisabeth. *Anna Freud: A Biography, 2nd ed.* London: Yale University Press, 2008.

Printed in the United States
by Baker & Taylor Publisher Services